PAIN IS MY COMPANION

A Professional Athletes Story
Russell Langhammer's Memoir

STEVE KRAVETZ

Copyright ©2024 Steve Kravetz and Russell Langhammer

No part of this work may be reproduced, stored in the retrieval system or transmitted in any form, or by any means, electronic, Mechanical, photocopying, recording, or otherwise without prior permission in writing from the author or publisher.

ISBN: 9-780-9996355

Published by Steve Kravetz

Cover Design jonathanshih@fiverr.com

Preface

This is a quote from a hematologist who understands chronic pain better than most doctors and specialists: "Chronic pain patients hide it so well, you can't go by how they look on the outside. They have to learn how to function with pain, you can't just roll around on the floor all day screaming in agony. Medical personnel in hospitals don't even realize this. A chronic pain patient can function with a pain level that would incapacitate any other person."

Dedication

To My Celsa, who has supported me through everything bad and shares with me everything good.

Table of Contents

Introduction 1
Chapter 1: In the beginning or First Pain 3
Chapter 2: New Home, New Life, New Name 7
Chapter 3: Then Sports and My Coach 10
Chapter 4: Out of Thin Air 13
Chapter 5: A Promised Kept 17
Chapter 6: Childhood Dream Accomplished 23
Chapter 7: Competing 29
Chapter 8: Pleasure 32
Chapter 9: The Good, The Bad, The Ugly 35
Chapter 10: Party Time and Opportunity 40
Chapter 11: New Additions to My Life 42
Chapter 12: New Beginnings and An Ending 46
My life in photos 49
Chapter 13: Dangerous Work 130
Chapter 14: I See a Bright Future 134
Chapter 15: Decision Time 136
Chapter 16: Clean 138
Chapter 17: And Then 139
Chapter 18: The Famous and Infamous 145
Chapter 19: The Downside 148
Chapter 20: My Reality 153
Chapter 21: My New Life's Purpose 155
Endocannabinoid system 157
The Final Chapter 162
Other books by Steve Kravetz 163

Pain Is My Companion

A Professional Athlete's Story

Life Story by: Russell Langhammer

With: Steve Kravetz

On January 3, 2019, at exactly 7:18 pm, I died.

Moments before I was alive, sitting at my kitchen table, chewing on a steak. Hurriedly scrolling through my Facebook account. Nothing new.

Bam, the next thing I know. I am in the middle of a field, feeling just a slight breeze across my body, and the most incredible calming feeling of wellbeing washing over me. This new feeling fills my body and mind. "This is awesome." I think to myself. "I have never experienced anything so peaceful in my whole life." As I looked up, my fixed glaze is now centered just outside the tree line. There, waving at me are two figures, of course I recognize them. It is my mother and younger brother Ricky. Each is trying to tell me something which for some reason I can't quite understand. I tried to hear what they were saying, but for just a second. I then looked over in time to see my beloved German grandfather, my Opa, stepping out of the woods.

"Nein, Rusty this is not your time, you must go back, Ver-Stay."

"No," I reply. "I love it here, I feel no pain OPA, I want to stay."

I was in mid-argument when my pacemaker shocked my heart back. I awoke pissed off and, in more pain than I had ever experienced or thought possible. My eye lids hurt. My anus hurt. There was not one item of my being that did not scream in pain. Lying on the floor, bowels emptied and nose running. Good or bad, I knew I had experienced something very few people would ever experience. This all happened in just a mere ninety-two seconds. Looking back in just a blink of an eye I had the most educational experience I have ever had.

Reality and pain were now forcing me to make a real-life choice. I could just lay here on the cold wood floor and maybe really die. I was not afraid of death now for I knew what awaited me on the other side. Or I could fight to live. My inside decision maker already had made up my mind for me. I was looking around for my phone and in my vision to my right, reaching out, was a strange hand and it was shaking so hard I thought *it must be on fire.* "Whose hand is that?" I am thinking. The hand seems to have a mind of its own. Which now was trying to control my destiny. I just stared at it. What was happening looked like I was just seeing the action from far away. My phone somehow was in that stranger's hand. I watched it begin to push buttons. A please SEND HELP message was sent out on my social media site. I was feeling so much pain and was wishing I had not come back. Thankfully several of my friends stepped up and after what seemed like years the Fire Department and Ambulance did show up. This was to be my first of the twenty sixth times in the hospital I would find myself during the year 2019. The last trip ended up with me having open-heart surgery to replace five valves and all the connected veins and arteries between them.

Looking back, I guess you could say, pain has been my companion for as long as can remember.

Chapter 1

In the beginning or First Pain

How did it start?

I was born Russell Langhammer at 11:55pm on April 10th, 1965, on a military air transit plane returning from Rhein Main AFB in Germany back to the United States. I was 11 pounds 7 ounces, and way too big for my mother's birth canal. They had to break my collar bone for me to be delivered mid-flight. This was the beginning of my journey with pain.

While at Womack Army hospital at Ft. Bragg I was also diagnosed with spinal meningitis that I had acquired somehow in just a few short hours. Two strikes in less than 48 hours against my new life. Mom's military Doctor told her, "I am sorry Mame, but your baby probably will not make it." What he could not have known, I had the Langhammer will, to survive. Even at only two days old. There is one thing for sure and that is, we Langhammer's are generational survivors.

My family on both sides are German's. The Langhammer's family were made up of many generations of military men, warriors, and fanatics about their country, on both sides.

My father was born in August of 1933. Raised in a strict home. Though he did not want to, he was forced to join the Hitler youth movement to help, as Germanies last hope.

My father though was born under a lucky star. In 1944, during an Allied bombing raid of Frankford. My dad's love for animals, in this case a cat named Bo-bo, saved his life. The Nazi's were in the streets killing stray animals. Dad, saw Bo-bo out meandering nearby, pop ran downstairs out the front door. He bravely rescued the cat from the rifleman up the street. Then even before he could turn around to head back to his home. Their entire building was blown to pieces by a stray allied bomb. Leaving a desolate heap of rubble. He had been home alone, and if not for love of animals he and Bo-bo both would have been killed. Bo-Bo by the Nazis prowling animal killers out that day and him in the shattered walls of the building.

My mother's side of the family are Jewish, from Geisingen and Steige/ Baden-Württemberg Germany. Huesman was their name before they had changed to Huesmann with the help of lots of cash, they got illegal identity papers. They were in the appliance business and part of the family had a delicatessen restaurant.

My Grampa Wilhelm Huesmann had been a well-known and quite famous professional Boxer in his younger days. When war came to Europe, he volunteered to join Spain's Army rather than be forced to be a Nazis.

During the war Wilhelm flew a specialized plane, call Airboats for the Spanish army, an Ally of Germany at the time. These specialized planes were used fly into ports of Spain's territories, where some did not have runways for an airplane to land but lots water. Unfortunately for him his plane was shot down while flying over England though he landed his plane, his wounds were too severe, and he died from them.

My grandmother was beside herself over his death. She let it be known that she blamed Hitler and the Nazi's for destroying Germany and the death of her husband. At a public rally she shot the middle finger at Hitler and called him out. She was arrested in 1944 along with my mom and her little brother Gerhardt. All three were sent to Bergen-Belsen concentration camps. Not as Jews, though they were, but as political dissenters, or as the German government spun it. My poor old grandmother was stirring up and spreading DEFEATISM.

My mother was a young girl when she was forced into barbwire confines. Living with hundreds of other lost souls, just trying to make it through another day. Harassed and threatened daily, it would leave such a scar on her she would never fully recover even as an adult.

My grandmother would only say, "she worked deals "with the guards to get extra food. When I asked her in my naivety, what did she mean, "worked deals" She would just repeat, "I worked deals to make sure we all survived." Today I understand, she did what she had to for her family.

Fortunately, a few of the family that did manage to escape, found their way to Argentina, Cuba and Australia. Mom, her uncle, and my grandmother survived and were rescued by American troops, in 1945. None of this side of the family would talk of their experiences, but from bits and pieces I know it was hell on my mother, she would attempt suicide three times during her lifetime. Her insecurities would show up in some of her crazy behavior and decision-making skills, all her life.

Interesting side note. In the 1930's the Huesman family, Grams and Grandfather Wilhelm, were on vacation in Puerto Rico and met a young baseball player called Hank Pete aka Pee-Wee Reece. A well-known short stop for the New York Dodgers. My grandfather and Pee-Wee became close friends and plan to start a Sports TV station after the war. Pee-Wee was instrumental in getting my mom and her family into the United States after the war. To Louisville Kentucky where he was from.

Just after the WW-2 the US government conducted a covert operation called: Operation Paperclip that brought back to America some of Germany's top Scientists, Engineers, and Technicians, and their families. The Russians did the same thing. In, 1958 My father and his brother came to the United States through Operation Paper Clip that way. My dad was 25 years old when he arrived, and the next year after receiving his citizenship he enlisted in the Army. He was sent back to Germany to train on Chinook Helicopters. His brother Rainier joined the United States Air Force the same day.

One day in 1963 my dad was sitting at a table in Augsburg Germany Officers Club when a lightning bolt hit him directly in his heart. She was a beautiful sweet-looking brunette, selling cigarettes to the officers in the club. The only reason he got a second glance back from her was dad had not been like all the other GI's. That every day were hitting on her. He was a gentleman in a European way plus dad obviously spoke perfect German. She was nineteen, the year was 1964, she was looking for security in her life. She thought my father could provide that security. They eloped to

Paris and only nine months later they would be parents of a big bouncing boy. ME.

My father was a helicopter pilot in Viet Nam, first in 1966 flighting in Chinooks, then again in 1968 this time Huey's were his tools. Dad's last tour was in 72, flying Cobras. Afterwords he went to work for the CIA. Flying drugs from central America to Air Force Bases in Florida to get cash for the Contra to pay for guns, which he then flew back. Working with the famous Lt. Colonel Ollie North.

We hardly saw him during those five years, she never felt secure with him always being gone. 1970 after his third tour, she could see the handwriting, so after my brother Ricky was born. They got a divorce. We then moved to Louisville Kentucky.

Chapter 2

New Home, New Life, New Name

Shortly after we arrived my mother was introduced to a gay mortician who eventually ran Cottrell Funeral Home in Butler County Missouri. At the time in order to be the Counties Mortician, required the person holding the office, to be married. Thus, he was eager to acquire a ready-made family. His name was Herbert Miller aka Blue. Mom this time was only looking for security and some peace, not love. She made us take his last name. So, from 1971 through 1983 I was known as Rusty Miller.

Blue and his family were tied to the KC Mafia. They had paid for Herberts schooling and needed him to cover this job as Butler County mortician and to run their funeral home. Part of Blue's job occasionally entailed disposing of their dead bodies. Blue's bosses also dealt in all kinds of drugs, gambling, and loan sharking.

The KC's family, our sponsor too now, also owned the flower shop across the street from the funeral home, which my mom ran. The two businesses were also used to launder the mob's cash. Plus, the shop also was used for drug drops while making the regular floral business deliveries.

My mother was quite a beautiful woman but had many of her own problems. Alcohol, and cocaine, to name a few, plus her own issues with sex addiction. She equated Sex with Love, and she was always looking for love.

I found myself from the age of eight on having to fighting off sexual advances by Blue and his many sick pedophile friends and his own family. I caught Blue and his boyfriend, who was a Captain in our Police department, in the middle of sex, one day. I was now able to use what I had seen too black mail them both to be free of that threat. I was young, but my instincts were right on. From that time on to even today, I can spot those sick predators and it always brings back a sickness deep in my gut.

From 1970 through 1981 life was pretty smooth, at least there was a lot of money in the house, mom had my half- brother Randy Miller.

My younger brother Ricky and I had always had a love-hate relationship. Where I had been able to outmaneuver Blues and his sick families' sexual advances, he was too young. Receiving the kind of attention he did not want but was unable to prevent. Thus, a lot of his inward anger was directed toward me. When we got into it as boys do, he was full steam ahead, and despite our size differences he was like a badger and never gave up. One time he shot me in the back with a 22 rifle, the little son of a bitch, broke one of my ribs. For some reason my mother was totally oblivious of it all. No surprise he became an alcoholic and drug addict in his early teens.

It was during this period my mom began getting loose. Blue was gone most of the time, so she and a new girlfriend Nancy. They would go out dancing, bar hopping, an as the old song says, **"looking for love in all the wrong places."** They would bring these guys home and have wide open door, wild sex. Sometimes I would take all the kids out for a midnight car ride, so they did not have to hear or see that adult activity.

Nancy had a son just a bit younger than me, Dale. For a time, we were tight.

Summertime and we were out of school, so you would find us on the way to or coming back from some hole with water. One morning a small group of guys headed out to Current River. Just a short bike ride. At one point there was always the challenge to jump off Bass Rock. It was not really a rock but rather a ledge that protruded out over the very fast running river. I was the new guy, so I volunteered to do it. I had my tennis shoes on, no big deal. Wrong, first I had to climb to the top of this very tall bluff even before I could get to the path down to Bass Rock. That old white rock was tightly packed in some spots but other times I take a step up and the rock ground under me would simply crumble. I am beginning to regret my choice. Nevertheless, I move forward and after finally getting to the top, the rest of the guys are now down at the river's shoreline, waiting on me. Yelling encouragement and dares. The trail down to Bass Rock is more complex than getting up to the top. Once there, I really began to regret my choice. I turn to climb back out when I realize the path has been designed for access but no regress. Unless I was a lizard there was only one way off that cliffside. As a slight breeze pushed me toward the edge. Slowly I scrapped up my courage and yelled**,** *Ohhh, Shiiiittt.* All the way down. I hit the water like a ton of bricks and just in a moment got my mouth shout before hitting the fast-running concrete hard water. The second I hit the surface it sucked me down and shot me across the river's bottom. I heard the sound of rocks being pushed against each other, The waters roaring also filled my ears. I dared not open my eyes but began to worry. I could not just push myself off the bottom. The water's weight was more than I expected, and it was hard enough not to explode from just holding my breath. I am thinking, "I am going to die, here and now." I began praying and making promises. Like a hand pushing me up, I found my head bobbing above the waters line. Finally, I found a tree root to grab onto it. Looking way back at the ant size people I had just left a few dozen moments ago. This maybe the first time I faced death, and it opened my eyes, but it did not make me any smarter, yet.

Chapter 3

Then Sports and My Coach

I found sports or maybe sports found me. In those days my routine consisted of my getting up at six in the morning, mounting my bike and meeting up with my friend Miky Shelton. We then would stop at the IGA to buy chocolate milk and a fried pie before we would head off to ride all over town, smoking stolen cigarettes, feeling our seed. It was on one of these early morning rides that found us smoking behind the football stadium.

"What are you fellows up to this early in the morning? Looking to start, working out, are we?"

This was my introduction to *purposeful exercise*. The questions were being asked by Coach Gayle Kingery, the high school's head football coach.

Every year he would take the bottom of the barrel kids or *at-risk kids*, that is what they would have called kids like me today. He would mix them into work out routines with older classmates, usually from the more affluent families and the middle-class kids who made up most of the squad. Rich kids sweat mixing with the rough around the edge types, like me. In the weightroom, all that counted was how hard you worked out. First period every morning, and if it was not raining, we were running after the weight room. If it was raining it just meant more time lifting steel and pushing yourself.

Coach Kingery and his wonderful wife took me into their lives. Mrs. Jolene Kingery was also a teacher but so much more. Jolene opened her home's doors and their heart to me. At this time in my life, the Kingery were the only normal people I knew. They each gave me a better view of life and what was actually possible.

Coach Kingery became my salvation, mentor, guide to adulthood. "Rusty, you have a natural ability, let's see if we can't put it to some good use." Coach knew what he was talking about too.

Sports became my escape. Coach Kingery showed me how to survive, to never, ever, give up, and his favorite, which was to be my motto, **"Pain is weakness leaving the body."** I started running track, high hurdles, then on to football. Weight training = strength, also equal pain, and sore muscles. It did not take me long to go from a skinny boney kid into a man's body. By the time I was fourteen I was his star athlete in track and field then onto football where I really excelled with his encouragement. Rusty he would say, "You have the ability to be a pro athlete and I'm going to ensure that you do to fill all your goals." I love that man and greatly respected him and his family even today, he is the one I report my success to.

There is another man who came into my life later and was also influential in my growth. Since Blue was hardly ever around those days, and their marriage at this point was just a total sham. My mother dated other men. Her boyfriend at the time was also my baseball coach Ed Randell. He was an awesome teacher and guided me back into sports. When I was twelve, I quit sports for a while. As a young adolescent I really needed direction. I started playing catcher for him and was really quite good, fast around the bases and I had a rocket arm. I was also able to hit a ton of home runs for him. In the end though, baseball season began the same time track season started, and I really loved running and jumping those hurdles.In 1983 the old number 17 won State champion in the hurdles for my High School's track team.

Another of my mom's party friends was a beautiful Black woman who only dated white men. She too had a son who went to a different school. Kennett High school was our biggest rival which was just across the river from Popular Bluff where I played. His name was Boris Whitside, and he was also a star running back for his high school. Boris was my nemesis. If I had a 100-yard game, he would have had a 125-yard game that same week. If I scored two touchdowns, he would score three. Though in our playoff game against each other at the end of the year, I caught the last pass of the game, scoring the winning touchdown.

His coach was a fellow by the name of Larry Lacewell. He was Borises Coach Kingery. Coach Lacewell took a job at Arkansas State and got Boris a scholarship there. In college, once again we would compete. It would be years later we would reconnect, and a real friendship would develop. On many levels we had grown up in similar environments. We each had a crazy mom and a coach that made a difference in our lives.

Years later he told me, "Russell just your being out there, pushed me every week, knowing you were going to try to beat me, made me a better player."

"Funny you said that" I replied. "Your being out there pushed me too."

We still keep in touch after all these years, and my friend Boris has a very successful real estate business around Atlanta.

Chapter 4

Out of Thin Air

In my freshman year of college, one afternoon, a well-dressed man approached a group of us after football practice. "Say guys I am looking for some strong armed, sharp minded men who would like to make some good money? "His words caught my attention immediately. I have always been the type of person who would rather stay busy and work, than sit in front of a TV or radio.

"Who do we got to kill," I asked using my coolest swagger.

He smiled but gave no reply. "I work at the airport and need some muscles to unload and load freight. It pays…"

Airport I'm thinking, exotic places, short skirt stewardess, I am in, I say to myself.

Again, first to reply, I could not help myself. "When can I start?" This quirk of a meeting would be a pivotal event for my future, of course I did not know it then. I worked part time and full time in the airline industry from 1983 until 2006. I also earned a certification from The Universität Heidelberg Transportation International Law and Logistics school. America Airlines sent me to their Flagship University for Dangerous goods in transport, weight balance, dispatcher, ramp operation, which would get me a job as The International Crew Chief in years to come.

Our lives changed November of 1980. Blue had been caught having sex with a corpse and that was just the beginning of his, the mob's family, and Blues own sick brother's family. They are all still in prison, including now, my half-brother Randy.

One day my mom came by my girlfriend's house to pick me up, the other boys were already in the van, and she told us. "We are moving and not to worry everything will be alright." She just kept saying we would be alright. We headed to the airport. **Operation paper clip** kept up with everything we did. Ricky and I had to take a series of ASVAV skill tests every year, the government for some reason made us take it to see our progress.

We went to Germany for a couple of weeks staying with the Langhammer family. My youngest brother Randy could not understand why everybody talked so strangely. He did not understand German at all. It was my first language, so it was no problem for me. Ricky could understand it though he was not particularly good at speaking it. I had a blast, but I missed my friends, my lady, who I thought was my one and only. Though it would be Coach Kingery I would miss the most.

We ended up back in the states after a few months. We would now be living in Louisville, also back with my own name Russell, Rusty, Langhammer. A federal agent handed us each of our new ID's. Social security cards, Drivers licenses for those of us who drove. Even an insurance card from USAA insurance with my old/new old, name. on it.

I started a new high school and began playing sports. I did reach out to coach Kingery, and we still stay connected.

My senior year in high school just before graduation, Ricky put me in a real bind. He had been dating this girl Judy most of the year and for some reason he dumped her and started dating her best friend, Julie. Judy went crazy. Wanting revenge, she went looking for the largest man she could find, which turned out to be the school's custodian, a giant of a fellow. Judy filled his head with lies about how Ricky had abused her.

This began a series of events. The custodian hunted Ricky down in front of his school locker. "Judy told me what you do to her, I am her man now, so you meet me behind the building 3:35 no later, understand me?"

Ricky just looked up, the hall was full of onlookers, he simply replied. "Check with my brother Rusty, he will meet you and kick your dumb ass all over this campus." He turned and walked away. Shooting him the French salute.

The brute then went to the school's cafeteria looking for me and to say he was mad is an understatement. "Who is Rusty Langhammer," he yelled out.

A few of the girls pointed to me. He came up to me. I looked up from my chair. All I could see was lots of blue cloth before it came to a collar which sprouted a tree trunk neck, atop it was a big, blond-haired head, sat. "Your brother said you will defend your queer loving, woman beating families name. So, M/F meet me out back after school, 3:35."

"Why wait, let's just get this over, now?" Was my naive reply. The whole dining hall followed us out back, I remember squaring off, then nothing. When I came back to reality. The custodian was lying sprawled out on the ground, wearing a swollen eye, busted nose and huge lip, now bleeding profusely. The principal came out then. He took him to the infirmary and me back into his office. "Sit here. I will be right back." He said, then turned and walked back out. Finally, when the principal did come back in to his office, he had already gotten the custodian's story and the school's tattler's version. He knew I had not started the fight, and his own job was now on the line. A staff member trying to physically assault a student. Not the way he wanted to end his career.

"Rusty, are you ok?" He started. "You know fighting is not the way to deal with conflict...ya,ya,ya. He went on, "you are about to start a new life, a future with unlimited possibilities, ya, ya, ya" He spent ten minutes trying to feel me out and build me up. "I'll not putting this on your records, and you promise not to get that crazy again, Ok?"

It would be after I left the campus with a few friends that I found out what happened while I blanked out.

"Dude, you struck that old guy before he knew what hit him, he had just started to lift his fist and you went crazy on him."

"Yeah, Rusty, I have seen you get mad before, but this was primitive, you gave him a cave man beating."

"Yeah, you went Fred Flintstone all over him." We all had a big laugh, but it worried me about blacking out like that.

It was all over school the next morning. The custodian had been fired. Judy had been expelled from school, and I was now officially the school's bad ass. In the end, Ricky had not even showed up to see what I had to go through for him.

Ricky would later have a difficult adulthood as well. He became a skilled tool and die maker working for a General Electric sub-contractor. His company offered him a contract to go down to Mexico to help set up an electric motor plant for one of their suppliers. While there he met and fell in love with the plant owner's daughter. He was also a cartel boss, and the old man loved Ricky. Especially his connections, for Ricky grew up around lots of mafia guys who worked with Blue in the drug business. Before long, my adrenalin junky brother, was smuggling lots of powders, into Kansas City, St. Louis and of course back home to Kentucky. Returning to Mexico with suitcases full of cash back. Ricky being Ricky did not walk it across the border, nor drive it across. Being a Langhammer he flew across it, but he delivered it in a unique way. He would fly over the border with a pilot and jump out of the plane, and sky dive it down. He did this over 2000 times, never getting caught. Easy money, poor choices, too much sampling of product and by 2017 he was beginning to owe the wrong type of people, money.

He died on Father's Day 2017, from a drug overdose. Suicide or accident? Really did not matter, it dawned on me that day maybe the whole Langhammer family is cursed.

Chapter 5

A Promised Kept

After High School graduation in 1983, as promised, Coach Kingery got me a football scholarship. At Hannover College, where I played running back. Then after two years and graduating with an associate in liberal arts degree. Coach Kingery once again, true to his promise, had me set up with another scholarship to play football this time for the University of Louisville. Those next two years I learned what playing football was really all about.

I am sure it is written in the official coaches' handbook that certain things must be said and repeated daily to everyone on their team to hear. **"Remember gentleman. Pain is weakness leaving the body, so dig into to the pain, push yourselves and lastly enjoy yourselves out there today."**

What I was to find out early. Pain brought focus, and for every ounce of pain experienced I would equally feel pounds of pure pleasure. At least when the pain stopped hurting. I am not sure which I became more addicted to pain or pleasure. The physical efforts also had unintended side effects, my body grew, firmed up and was to become my own calling card. Coach Kingery told us, "Men you will learn more about yourself here in the weight room than anywhere else on earth."

I was in my freshman year in college when the first thing I noticed. These guys I am playing with were very, very, good. No second stringers here, and we were not going to be playing high school level ball. I spent a lot of time in the weight room and was the strongest guy on the team at least in that weight room. One day my strength coach approached me and asked if I was taking any steroids. "No," I told him never. I did not know anything about them. He told me to meet Dave after dinner that night. Dave was a former college football player who had gone pro. He gave me a bag full of pills and a bottle of some kind of oil and some needles.

"Take one blue pill before breakfast. The pink one at lunch and the white one at dinner. Get your roommate to give you these testosterone injections Mondays, Wednesdays, and Fridays. I started taking them for track and field then onto football where I really excelled, especially with his encouragement. "Rusty," he would say, "You have the ability to be a pro athlete and I'm going to ensure that you do all you can to fulfill your goals if you put in the extra effort, it takes to succeed." We had a Championship season that year. I am not bragging but just stating the true facts. I was a big reason for many of those games' successes, that year.

Though I must admit I was always bigger and stronger than anyone else on my team. Also I was lucky to have been born with **Langhammer's** great genes.

On and off the field. With all that was going on in my life. I was lucky to eventually graduate in 1987, with a BA in Business Management.

April of 1984 a fellow teammate of mine needed me to pick him up at the airport. His mother after a long bout with Cancer had passed and Allen had gone back to Chicago for the funeral. I had arranged free tickets for him, through work, knowing he was on a tight budget. Needless to say, he was in a poor mood when he arrived back at school. We headed to an old haunt, the Troubadour and rode mechanical bulls and got very drunk on cheap beer. At about 3:30 AM the place was nearly empty, so we headed out-the front door of the bar and gracefully as possible walked across the street to the 24-hour Kroger's. We together barely had the $4.00 cash for a case of cheapo, Meister Brau beer. On our way out of Kroger's a few folks recognized us and invited us to an LSD party. We ended up swapping a few beers for a couple of hits of acid. As we were leaving, a police cruiser passed us, and it was heading right for the group we had just left.

We each took the hit of Acid, washing it down with another beer. Next stop White Castle to cure our munchies. It was right off campus, a hamburger joint that was always busy. Allen's driving up till now was not a concern to me. He then circled the building and all of a sudden, he hit the brakes, stopping us dead in front of the big glass wall that looked out onto the parking lot. I looked over," "WTF dude, I just spilled my brew." I then followed his stare. In the front booth was his long-time girlfriend locking lips with some handsome Hollywood Mike type. He came home early, and she did not know it. The LSD was now just beginning to kick in. He went ballistic, lots of colorful and lots of old fashion cussing took place. The more the acid kicked in the more radical his verbiage became. Also, the funnier the whole thing became to us. We were both hysterical, we were nearly pissing ourselves with laughter. I suggested we come off the highway, and just cut through some side streets to avoid the police. I soon felt us speeding down a hill at 90 mph and when we hit the T bottom he turned hard right. I have no idea what he was thinking if anything. The morning's dew was a glaze over the ground covering everything with a fresh slick wet coating. We slid across the concrete street, over a curb, through a front yard, passed a big oak tree, right into the front porch of a house. The force somehow threw me out of the car, into the non-damaged part of the front yard. Allen broke his neck and was stuck behind the steering wheel. He was trying to start the truck when the ambulance and fire department showed up. I was in shock laying on the ground. The car was in a blaze, and I was tripping full time by now. The whole thing seemed so unreal, yet there it was, happening right in front of me. The car no longer had any wheels on, I never found out if it was the LSD or if they really were gone. Allen had to be cut out of his seat and we both were taken to Audubon hospital. We made the newspaper and because we were football players we did not get into any legal problems. The downside of the story, those carefree laughs we had, were to be Allen's last for a while, because he had broken his neck. The next few years he spent in rehab learning to walk again. He also had to wear a metal hallo device around his head to the top of his shoulders. The head piece was actually screwed into his skull. This was to prevent as little future damage to his spine until it fully healed. He used to joke that when they did finally remove the screws, he would look like Frankenstein screw holes and all. He lost his scholarship of course, but we were both lucky to have survived the crash.

The old girlfriend never knew she was the cause, when she heard he was in the hospital, she just moved on. Married a rich man and they jet set the world. Even today I am sure she never knew or would have cared.

The crazy price we pay for love.

Just before 1985 spring training season begun our new leader, Coach Schellenberger told us. "As of today, nobody here has a guaranteed scholarship. Each one of you has to earn your spot on this team for those scholarships." He also set up rules he expected us to follow off the field as well. "No gold or silver chains. No earrings or studs. If you have a tattoo, you have to totally cover it up." The biggest disappointment was the last rule, the one about this year's spring break. "It is cancelled, none of you are to leave town and no partying. "

One of the guy's girlfriends, Ann, was from Ft. Lauderdale. She had invited six of us to join her at her family's beach front house. Ignoring the rules, we took off in two cars. We had loaded up on booze and weed and headed south.

The first two days was crazy, we had women coming and going. Debauchery and lots of poor choices. On the third day Ann's mom woke us all up in the morning, banging pots together. "You animals must leave, NOW!

None of us had much cash and considered heading back home. We had pulled off the main road, away from the beach, toward the intercoastal canal. Just before we hit the water of the canal, I took a right onto the last street. There in front of me was a sign written in German. I pulled over and went into the office. A short crazy haired man came from behind the desk. "What'd you want?" He had sideburns and sounded like he was an Elvis Presley impersonator.

I took a double look at him and replied in German. I am Russell Langhammer and my buddies, and I are looking for a few reasonable priced rooms." We got to talking and it seems his motel catered exclusively to German visitors, except during spring break so he actual had empty rooms.

"How much can you afford," he asked?

"$25.00. for," Was all I got out of my mouth, when he looked up at me.

"Your friends are big like you?" Ya?"

I smiled, "yes, why?"

"Maybe we can work something out." We walked out to his parking lot." I get people who ignore my *No Parking Signs*, and it takes the wreckers hours to get here when I call. Can you guys pick the cars up and put them in the da street?

"Sure, with these guys, we pick up lots more weight every day in the gym." I turned and signaled the guys to help pick up the car that Mr. Wolfenstein pointed to.

"You guys take care of my parking problem this week and you can have the rooms."

The next three days were a blast. That weekend we played football on the beach against a group football player from Ohio State. The Playboy Channel was in town and filming for their channel. They filmed much of the game and the drunkenness that followed.

We all went to a local mall one afternoon and ended up getting our ears pierced. The week went by way too fast and Wolfie was a great host, and he got a thrill every time we picked up a car or truck and moved it to the middle of the street.

It was only after we snuck back into town, we realized the reddish tint we had on our skin might be noticed. I missed my first two morning classes and was trying to lie low. I was crossing the edge of campus when someone grabbed my ear from behind.

"Just the man I was looking for." Coach Ganong had spotted me, and I was about to pay for my sins. "Follow me Mr. Langhammer." That would be harder than I cared for, because he never let go of my ear. He just pulled me across campus. I was pushed into his office, where I found the other five guys. "Guess what I saw last night on **MY** TV? I'm looking for bunny tits and ass, but I see you six. Things being bad enough that you broke our rules, but you also risked your bodies playing sand football and in doing so, risking injuries. You would lose your scholarships all for a short thrill. You could also have put your teammates in a big bind too. The only rule you guys did not break was having gold or silver chains. So, bring your sunburned bodies and meet me in the stadium and take those dam earring out."

We spent the next six hours running up and down the Colosseum steps with our helmets on. Row after row after row. Getting short breaks only for water, and five-minutes rest every ninety minutes or so. I don't think I have ever been so tired. In the end though, each one of the six of us ended up having our best years ever. So maybe the break did-do us some good.

Chapter 6

Childhood Dream Accomplished

1986, in the second to last game of our season, my college football careers ended., We were playing Indiana State, I blew out my knee. I needed good knees if I was going to get a chance to get drafted into the pros. I had orthoscopic knee surgery right away and started rehab sooner than I probably should have. It caused me a lot of physical pain but also heart break. The pressure would be on only me; would I be ready for the draft; my **childhood dream** was to play Professional Football. I was back at the gym, and the pain grinded.

John Wooten at the time was working for the Dallas Cowboys as a talent scout. He was touring certain colleges throughout the country looking for hidden talent. John approached me one day and made his pitch.

"Listen Russ, guys like you win a spot-on team's all the time, even after not getting picked up in the draft. Tell you what, the Cowboys are having a three-day event, it is geared for walk On's, like yourself. Here is my card, it will be your ticket in. The first day is a flood of guys, so come the second day. The coaches will be more open, give you more time to review."

"What about the third day," I asked, smiling?

"No, those are usually the over the hill group or rejects from someone else's event." He chuckles and shakes his head." Second day, see you there." John repeated as he walked away.

I did show up the second day of try outs, I had to get a physical on my own dime, but the team provided everything from shoes to helmets and everything in between.

I busted my ass and ignored my knees pain. I owe John a big thank you, and he was 100% right. The second day the coaches were more attentive. Spending more time with the backup quarter backs, receivers and running backs, like my-self. At the end of the 1987 camp, I walked away with my first professional athletic contract. I was a Dallas Cowboy. At least my knees were under contract as long as they held up. I have never been prouder than the first time I came to *my* locker. Printed on the front of the door is **R. Langhammer**. I had made it just like coach Kingery promised.

I'd gotten my dream, but I had taken a risk, because I was still in the transportation workers union, and I was not sure how the Chicago bosses were going to take it. I worried someone might appear and ask me to play poorly or fumble the ball. It would turn out they were proud, and I never got any special request, except for free tickets.

In my class that year were Bill Bates and Marc Tuinei. They both were very helpful. Tuinei and I hung out some. His Hawaiian and Samoan friends here in the area were gym rats too. I got to know a little about their culture, as warriors, and big-time party animals. Unfortunately, even then, Mark had a problem with drugs, especially heroin. It would be his downfall and bring him an early death.

The first year's season lasted only two games before the league went on strike. I spent an additional two years with the team as a red shirt. Or as a glorified tackling dummy for the A-team. When the new management came in, I was traded to the New England Patriots. The move for me turned out to be a big mess. Soon, after I showed up, I hurt my leg again.

My days of running down the field with the ball in my hand were over. It was a bitter piece of reality. As Coach Kingery would have said, "**In the end, like it or not, being fair or not, we are still stuck with reality, like it or not. Deal with it.**"

I knew I needed something else physical to do to keep from going crazy and to feed my need for the endorphins. In 1990 I took up bodybuilding and powerlifting. Soon after I was competing worldwide. It was simple, me against myself, against the pain.

Bodybuilding, in reality, is a terrible sport. Extremely dangerous, diet, drugs, hard training, and crazy eating habits. Again, it was me against myself, a road to self-destruction. Soon after I got my cherished Pro-Card success came to me when I became APFA TEXAS 242-pound champion.

Steroids especially, are extremely hard on your body but it also screws with you mind and thinking. The longer I took them, I found It was becoming increasingly more difficult to control my emotions like anger.

Not that I ever had an inferiority complex, but narcissistic behavior also began showing up in my persona.

F/U either you loved me or not. Durning those years I traveled extensively for work and to compete internationally. Which lead to my having multiple girlfriends, like a sailor, I had a girl in every port. Airport that is. One in Germany, Mexico, Austria, Hungary, Venezuela.

I do not know if it was the drugs or what, but after a rainy weekend I spent inside watch old war movies. I decided I needed to change course in my life. I needed to join the family's occupational tradition. Join the Army and fly aircraft. I came from it honestly. My Great Grand Father Langhammer, his son my grandfather and my father plus his brother, my uncle all flew for their Military during conflict. My Mothers Father too flew for the Spanish Army. Monday morning, I was at a local recruiting office sitting across the desk from Master Sargent Sampson. I told my story, he just stared back at me. I could see a little fire in his eyes.

"Mr. Langhammer, I believe I can help you fulfill your destiny. He reached into his desk, pulled out some paperwork which he quickly went over." Sign here, sign here, and again here and there. Great, I will phone you as soon as I can set you up to take the needed ASVAB'S first.[st.] These are the army's version of IQ, Personality, and Educational Competence test. Plus, they also do a full background check. All this was geared toward eliminating the crazies, the physically unfit, or those who would not make very good soldiers, or could not follow orders, kinds of soldiers.

I had no sooner got home than the phone started ringing. "Mr. Langhammer can you be here at my office at eight hundred tomorrow. I have arranged for a tester to be here to administer all your tests except the physical. Your background check came out blue chip, as I had expected it would. After all your father being Colonel Langhammer and all. I am sure he is enormously proud."

The mention of how my dad might feel brought anxiety. I had not even called him to discuss this idea. He had to know by now through the military grape vine. I quickly got on the phone to reach out to him. I left my message and hoped he was going to be happy or at least proud.

From eight that morning till one that afternoon, I had one test after another. My brain was numb when I left that recruiter's office.

My dad called me back the next morning. He did not pull any punches. Telling me of some of the horror stories he had participated in. He gave me a really fast education on what I can expect.

"Thank you pop for your truthful Insite, I just wanted to make the family proud."

"Just make yourself proud Russell, the rest will take care of itself." Was his parting comment.

My guide, Sargent Sampson, called that my physical was set up in Louisville's Federal Building. The army set up airline tickets, a hotel room for the night and a ride in an Army green bus to the building where the physical exam would be held.

If I thought the mental test were numbing, these were invasive. First, they took all the fluids I had for testing. Then from the top of my head to the bottom of my feet and every open and closed orifice in my body was inspected.

After I dressed, I was directed into the head Doctor's office. He was a full bird Coronel, like my dad. I am feeling good. My body had never looked better. I felt great, and thought, "I am going to be the next poster boy for the **New Army.**"

"Mr. Langhammer I am afraid the United States Army must reject your application at this time, I am sorry."

His words hit me between my eyes, what did he just say. I was rejected. "Are you crazy Sir, why would **You** pass on me?"

"It is your heart, surely you know, after being a professional athlete and all. I am not the first Doctor to tell you this, I'm sure. Your heart is enlarged. So much so we could not afford to have you flying anything. That is just the way it is. I suggest...."

I did not hear the rest of his speech. I just walked out.

I totally blanked the news out; I was competing in a Bodybuilding competition the next weekend anyway.

Dad never said anything, but I got a strong feeling he was relieved, I did not have to be a soldier.

I too was relieved later when I calmed down from being so mad at not making it. Let's just say. "What the hell was I thinking." Spending years being told what to do, and where and when to do it. I would have hated it, so my being rejected turned out to be a blessing for me. It also made me aware of my oversize heart problem. Doctors later would tell me they thought it had been caused when I had gotten spinal meningitis as a newborn.

My dad was not around much in my youth, especially after they got a divorce. When I got into college, and started playing football, I would see him more often. He relished my success, and often brought some of his CIA, spook friends to watch. In the late 80's we often met at the airport as he might be passing through. We would always have lunch.

There is in February, a carnival called Fasching, in Germany, he and I begin going together for several years. It was the Germans version of Marti Gras held in Colon. Fresh Pretzel, hot sausages and Klapfer. Germany version of Jelly donuts, and of course lots of beer were the food specialties of the fair. We had lots of time celebrating with our older German side of the family. Spending those few days here and there would become our time to really connect and get to know each other better.

In 1992 the Viet Nam War Memorial was opened, and he asked me to join him. The area around this site is remarkably busy and quite loud. When we stepped down into the actual wall area, it was dead silent. My father took me over to one name.

"See this name, *Euless Gregory*, he was one of my best friends. He was fearless. When we were taking enemy fire he would jump on the m-60, hanging out the door, firing back at the enemy, who were raking us with ground fire. We had landed and loaded up a few wounded men. This time was different. I had just swung up and tilted away when just a lucky sniper shot rang out. That son of a bitch killed him with that one shot."

He took out a piece of paper and using a lead pencil traced his name. I have only seen my father cry once and it was that day. He said truly little after that but repeated the jester for at least six more names. That night we partied with several of his CIA friends. They all had seen action like my dad, they had lots of stories and as the night went on it got more and more morbid. I am glad I got to share this experience with him, even if it was not fun, or joyful, it was still shared time.

Chapter 7

Competing

In the late 1980's, Body Building and its commercial competition was an infant stage. In the Dallas Ft. Worth area. It was ruled by an old Queen, Marvin Meinstein. He approached me and asked if I might be interested in competing in his league. Ronnie Colman, Mr. Olympian eight times, was in this league, so I agreed. He wanted to start by doing a photo shoot. I showed up at his house with the most beautiful stewardess Lisa who I was dating at the time. Marvin was pissed off right away. He had been hoping for a little play from me. "Here put these on," he said as he handed me the G. "You can change here." I ignored him and changed in the bathroom. I refused to do nudes. During all those years I have done five or more body building magazine spreads, like I did for **Muscle and Fitness**, and lots of promo shots. None in the nude.

The industry has many homosexual men, and too many pedophiles who seem to hang out around the edges. Looking for naive pretty want-to-Be's, in their teens. I have been around these men since I was six years old and can spot them a mile away. Man, sex has never been an interest of mine, but I believe each to his own. As long as it's not forces or coerced. Over the years competing, or at work, in life I have had gay friends. In the end, after all, we are all just looking for acceptance.

The world of Power Lifting though is where you compete one on one with just yourself. The steel which hangs on a bar does not care. It is just dead weight, and it is your only opponent besides yourself. You can physically pick the Ferris bulk, lift it off the floor, up to the chest and then over your head. It is a lot harder than it looks. The answer comes fast when it becomes your turn. A simple and quick: YES, or No. No politics, no special sexual favors. DO it or NOT do it.

Body Building on the other hand had lots of back-room politics, like wrestling. As a competitor you are competing against other men. Judges whose idea of a perfect body may or may not be like yours. The judging has guidelines but, in the end, it is all in the eye of the paid beholder.

Reality is, and this is not the first time I have said this in public, Body Building is a terrible sport. It is hard on your body of course but your mind as well. If a man or woman is on a stage anywhere in the world competitively competing, they have had steroid drugs in their regiment. I began taking them in college while playing football.

Old time body builders like Arnold Schwarzenegger, and Eight-time world champion, Ronnie Coleman, even with being born with great genetics and having put in lots of work have not gotten that way without chemical help. These guys and other old timers set the work out standards for all serious contenders.

Prior to the 17 weeks of work out prep before a major competition, we would put on as much weight as possible the rest of the year. In the beginning of February, I would go to Germany. I would eat schnitzel, pasta, potatoes, rice, pork, chicken. Anything with lots of protein. An of course lots of Dark German Beer. Anything with protein was consumed, including a Pro- Drink called Met/rx which had originally been developed for Aids patients who were not consuming enough protein due to lack of appetite. Now a big part of the body builders building blocks. Which need lots of amino acids, minerals, and whey type proteins. I would eat everything that was not tied down, plus pounds of supplements every day I would put on 50 pounds or so, then come home bloated almost unrecognizable.

The next seventeen weeks were devoted to carving that bulk weight down and to push it into growing new muscles where we wanted them. I would go from 10,000 calories a day, prior to, then when training started only having 1800 calories a day. And the training was all out. I would live in a state of exhaustion and hunger for each of those 24-hour days. Days that turned into months of competition.

Losing as much weight over a short period of time. To turn as much of it as possible into strong bulk. This was done with the help of drugs, which we got from greedy Veterinarians. Yes, large animal strength steroids and performance enhancing substances. It made us look like comic book monsters, which was what the sport required. Meanwhile the drugs also would make our personalities change into those same cartoon monsters. Short tempers quickly could turn into rage over nothing.

What harm all this did to our bodies would show up later, unfortunately not too much later.

Before each show we all get worked up, slapping the shit out of each other, sniffing ammonia to get mad, raise our hormone levels. I never needed anyone to hit me. Just a quick flash back to some of the memories from my childhood was enough to get me worked up ready to kick someone's ass.

The judges are looking for Symmetry and Balance for each of the muscle groups. Head, neck, the full shoulder muscle group. The chest, arms, back abdomen thighs and calves. Each class is judged and when all done the totals are tallied. The first-place winner has the fewest points. I did have my share of placing in these events. Lots of third place wins.

The judges were paid to evaluate, each had things that were important to them to see. But reality was-- Politics/ Business, = $,000 and these promotors were in this for the long play. So, on more than one of these stages the winner was already chosen before the doors even opened. There were good guys and bad guys like wrestling, with just a bit less pomp and glitter. They wanted the long-time rivalries to bring in larger crowds.

Chapter 8

Pleasure

Pushing freight was not the only part time job I had in college. Wednesday nights I worked as a server at, **The Toy Tiger**, a male strip club for ladies only. I'm making good tips, and the place was full of fun. One night the manager came up to me. "Russ, I need you to fill in for, Johnny Be Good, the dumb ass fell of his bike and broke his leg. Go in the back oil up and grab a clean G, you'll be new meat for the ladies, beside you should pick up at least a grand tonight." He turned and walked away. I am not shy, and the attire or lack of it as servers is not much different than the performers. After a bit of liquid courage and a big fat dobie, I was **"The Man"** I don't know how I looked from the ladies sitting their point of view staring up at the show of fresh meat. I did not care, for I was doing my best to ripple the muscles, wag the tail, and flap my loosely cover cock in more than one lady's face. I have never felt so free, and desirable.

Sure, enough I did make over a grand that night and left with more than one available female phone number. Wednesday nights I would become a regular performer. Then I started working Saturday nights at private parties through a group we called, **For Your Eyes Only**.

I was living the life of Hugh 'the fockin' Hefner. Great sex that I was being paid for, some of the best pot money could buy. All my entertainment, clothes. A car, my pad, all being paid for by alumni, or by one of my ladies.

Sex, with women, girls, and MILF's, was to become a second addiction. I lost my virginity when I was quite young on the hood of a Corvette with a friend of my mother's.

After that I never looked back. Being an athlete, the female species flocked to me like I was giving gold away not just a few hours of pleasure. "Practice makes perfect," the coach used to say. So, I practiced every chance I could, and it sure beat the weight room work outs. Plus, sometimes I would make good money too, as an occasional Gigolo.

Now saying that, like every sport there are women. Muscle loving women. Each Gym had them. Most were very fit themselves. Lot of wild, untethered Orgies at gyms like Stroud Gym were to be had all around the country. Lots of Ecstasy, lots of sweaty raw sex.

Big muscles though also give some people the wrong opinion of us. One night I was working the lounge at the airport when three Stewardess from a Lufthansa fight came in to kill some time. My back was to them, but I heard one of them say in German. "Look another muscle head, lots of big ones on the outside, but just a tiny one between their legs." The three girls just broke out in laughter.

I just turned and with a big smile on my face, replied in my best German. "Ladies you should not judge a book just by its cover. In my case the one that counts for you all, is bigger than your favorite Bratwurst." I simply turned and walked away. I had embarrassed them and when I brought each of the three a complimentary drink, well that opened a line of communication. It also would bring me to my first foursome.

In early 1988 I was having lunch in Chilies by myself. When a very beautiful Mediterranean looking woman approached me. "Excuse me sir, may I sit down?"

I had a mouth full of food, so I just nodded and quickly gulped down my contents.

"Russell Langhammer," I extended my hand. "You look familiar, but I am not sure from where?" This is my standard line when I meet someone I may or may not know.

"Nippy, you may know me from my photo spread in Penthouse, Russell." She looked deep into my eyes. Russell. "I am from the West Coast with my investor, Doc." She pointed over to another table where a well-tanned middle-aged man sat. He smiled and lifted his drink to me. "We are here to open a branch of exclusive dating service. One for women with **needs** and **wants,** you know what I mean. They pay us for dates with handsome men like yourself. We have opened several clubs across the country. Now we are here in Dallas/ Fort Worth. Would you be interested in working as our spokesperson?"

She continued with her pitch. "Women pay a monthly fee, the more they pay the more parties they can attend." It would bring me one of the craziest few months of my life. These women paid hard cash to attend her parties [**Orgy's**] on weekly bases and for $X,000 a one-on-one date. Most of the women who signed up were desperate and were paying for sex. The company they started also had same services for men. I brought in a few of my fellow male airline employees who too were equally hard up and were willing to paid for the club's services.

After only two weeks Nippy and I began having really passionate sex. "Russell, I love you so, don't you think we are soul mates? I do, and lover together we are going to make a ton of cash." During that time, I rarely saw Doc, thinking he was traveling to other offices.

Nippy reminded me of a young Sofia Loren and she definitely was a woman who knew how to use her whole body in totally different ways. She was open to trying anything. Each week the sex got better and better. I am seeing hearts.

Then one night out of the blue, I got a call from her. "Heah Russ, we are going back to the west coast, sorry, thanks for everything, good-bye." Followed by a quick click, no explanation. Just as soon as it had begun, she was gone and they disappeared. Like smoke in the night.

On the one hand I was living any red-blooded, horn dog of a man's, dream. On the other hand, deep down, it was all hollow. I would wake up the next day or so, and I would have had my physical needs serviced but deep down I knew I wanted more.

Chapter 9

The Good, The Bad, The Ugly

The Good:

Durning operations DESERT SHIELD AND OPERATION DESERT STORM, my crew and I worked lots of night shifts, at DFW airport. To work Cabin Service, basically cleaning and stocking the aircraft for the Military Charters to the Middel East. It did not take all night so some would take to the crew's rest beds. All of the wide body jets had them. The beds were used for quickies, fast relief, without having to get a hotel room. One night a Maintenance Foreman came to 747 SP for NRT {Tokyo] and found a lady engaged in sex with two men. He started screaming," FORNICATION...FORNICATION." He fell flat to his knees and had a heart attack right there in front of us. The Ambulance came and took him away. I have heard of people having heart attacks from having sex but never from just watching.

While working for American Airlines I always volunteered for MAKE A WISH FOUNDATION year-round, but especially around Christmas. This was when I would see some of the same kids every year and could see the improvement one or other child had accomplished. Knowing what kind of hard physical and mental work they had have done during the year to achieve their own successes. I played Santa Clause, the all-knowing. So, when I call the child by their name and praise them for doing such an excellent job and improving in this or that. It meant the world to them, because it was not just anyone who was giving them praise but Old Saint Nick himself. Years later I ran into a few of my old participants. The same words come out of each one's mouth. "Santa's visits and praises made the next year bearable and made Christmas so very special."

An actual flight, taking off circling the Dallas area and landing back at the same gate was also a big part of the visit. The kids would sit by the windows and be amazed to see areas that they could recognize. Once back on the ground the group would be greeted by elves who provided snow and a present for each of the kids. I had the Santa job for years, but the Mrs. Claus job changed every year. One particular year one of the oldest ladies in the corporate office won the opportunity to play Mrs. Clause. She took the role too seriously. At the reception, she pulled me into a storage closet and had her way with me.

I still get a warm positive feeling when Christmas time comes around, and truth be told, I still get a little chubby every time I see a lady dressed as an elf or Ms. Claus.

The Bad:

The biggest bodybuilding power lifting event of the year was coming up in Dallas so me and most of my muscle head friends were at the gym seven days a week, month in and month out. One morning in early June of 1994 one of the guys comes in an announces a FUNJET trip 3 nights 4 days in Puerto Vallarta Mexico all-inclusive vacation, for only $325.00 total. Six of us went down to blow off steam after so many hours in the gym. Fresh air, salt water, cheap booze, and lots of hot scenery. We had no sooner got on the resort's grounds and the women and gay guys go gaga. I went up to my room, unpacked and put my swimsuit on. Heading for the bar I bumped into a beautiful dark-haired beauty. "Heah handsome has anyone told you that your big blue eyes are burning their soul." She grabbed my hand and proceeded to pull me to a secluded spot on the beach and we spent the rest of the day in and out of the water without a stitch on. The only part of me not tan was sunburn. Yeah, even that part of me. I spent part of that evening soaking my ass in a tub of ice-cold water with vinegar added to pull the heat out of my previous pale, area which now was very red and burning like hot coals. The next morning, we guys ate a hearty breakfast then off we all went snorkeling in Los Arcos. Swimming with the fishes and observing some of mother nature's greatest works at least below the water. Beautiful fish swimming in little and big schools. Colors and patterns that just took my breath away. In and out of the corral they would glide by swimming one way and suddenly the whole group moved off in unison into another direction. I swam so easily and carefree, no pain, no worries.

The day was perfect when Tiger sharks began circling the area, we were currently in. I do not know if we were in their feeding ground, but all of us knew we did not want to be anyone of their dinners.

I was feeling dirty from the morning saltwater swim and sandy from the beach walking back. Heah I am thinking, why go all the way up to my room? I'll just jump into the big pool, get cooled off and cleaned at the same time. The pool was huge with a two-story diving board at one end and a swim up bar in another part of the pool. Not looking at where I was or where I was heading, I dove in face first. The part of the pool was in was a beach entry, the water was not feet deep but inches. My face hit first, knocking me clean out. One of my buddies reached down and pulled me out of the water. Otherwise, I would have drowned in the water or in my own blood, which now was pouring out of what was left of my smashed nose.

"Hammer you need to go to the hospital right now," he said.

I was so pissed at myself. How could I have been so stupid? I was sober as a church mouse and could not blame booze or drugs for this choice. "F-ck it, just do your thing and reset my nose here, now." He did with just one pull left and right, and then down.

The blood eventually stopped flowing and I still had two more days left of the trip. When I was not in bed asleep, I was at the bar drunk, or getting drunk. The minute we got back to Dallas I headed to the hospital even before I went home.

Good thing. The x-rays showed I had also shattered my cheek bone and cracked two bones in my neck. For the first time Mr. Superman was brought down from my high horse. I could have died, and I was lucky my fall has not been more sever.

Three months later I was on stage competing in my last bodybuilding competition. I was competing in the 220-pound division in power lifting, where I set two new records that year and then crowned 242-pound powerlifting champion.

The Ugly:

There were times when my job at the airline was not exciting, at least not the kind of excitement anyone wants. December 20th, 1995, America Airlines flight 985 from Miami to Cali Columbia was filled with 163 passengers and crew. The plane was full of families and individuals returning to Columbia to spend the upcoming holidays with friends and loved ones. Delays loading passengers in Miami and the hour sitting on the tarmac waiting to get to take off put the flight two hours delayed, leaving at 5:14 PM. Upon arrival more snap foo's. A simple landing becomes a nightmare. Misunderstood directions from the Cali tower put the pilots over unfamiliar mountains 35 miles east of the airport. At 9:45 the last transmission received by the tower. When after fifteen minutes with no reply, the airport notified the Columbian Airforce of the missing plane. There were no roads to the area, but they sent out that night a squad of rescuers by foot to climb the 10,000 ft heavily wood steep terrain. It would be morning before air recognizance could start. The ground rescue crew got to the site shortly after the first helicopter. What they found was a miracle. A father and daughter were found alive. One other man and another woman were also found alive. All had multiple injuries. There also was one dog who somehow survived the crash, unscaled.

I got a call the next day from work. "Russell head out to Miami, get on the next flight to Columbia. Work with our staff there. Then go off to the crash site. Find, recover, and put the US Government top secret paperwork and items shipped with those docs, into the right people's hands personally." The US government used airlines often to send their top-secret correspondence abroad.

The sweltering damp heat at the base of the mountain was bad enough, but the freezing cold temperatures at the crash site made everything that much harder. With the help of American Airline local employees help I was able to remove our assignment and deliver it to the correct people. It took me almost a full week to accomplish the job satisfactorily. Initially when we got to the crash site, two things struck me right away. First, was the stench of decaying bodies mixed with the aviation fuel which I had to inhale with each breath I took of the cold thin air. Second, all the dead were naked. No clothes, no jewelry, no luggage was to be found.

Within just a few days the locals were all wearing clothing I could tell was not from their area's merchants. I was told the locals came right after the helicopters left the area with the wounded. It had been a prayer answered for them. Now I am not naive, I seen lots of poor people back home in Kentucky while growing up, but it was here I found out what real poverty was. Tin roof, scrap wood sides, dirt floor dwellings, and those were the lucky ones. No running water and sanitation was behind some trees. Open fire cooking, smoke everywhere.

The Columbian Air force and agents from our FAA came in to investigate. I can't understand this at all. It makes no sense how could such a sophisticated airplane crash? The captain had been flying for over twenty years, ten of them flying into this airport. The aircraft was equipped with aviation's newest high technology radar, which was meant to stop accidents like this from ever happening. The black box was found and after months of investigating it was determined as pilot's error.

I knew that report was pure bull shit. I was so mad I reached out asking my dad for help to get the real truth. He, through his CIA connections, got me the answers I and the pilot's family were looking for. Dad told me It was a Columbian terrorist group called FARQ, who for decades had been at war with the legal Columbian government. This terrorist group had moved part of the airport's radar system to a new location. This caused false readings for 965 computers. The night was pitch black, no moonlight. By the time the captain realized their danger, it was too late. The official story did not change, but I made sure his family did know the truth, not that it brought them any real relief.

Chapter 10

Party Time and Opportunity

Kentucky is officially not a state, but rather a commonwealth. Which lends itself open to tons of corruption aka the mob. Whiskey, Weed, Women, and of course Gambling, = a money laundering heaven. The Kentucky Derby brought all that and more.

The Wednesday before the famous horse race there is another famous race the locals always love, and heavy betting can be seen up and down at the race site. It is called the Great Ohio Riverboat race. The steam ship American Countess, versus her rivals. Bell of Cincinnati and the twin sister The Bell of Louisville. Rain or shine, people show up. Many in 1800 colorfully garb, to cheer their steamboat champion on.

The Kentucky Derby is run on the first Saturday of May at Church Hill Downs. This horse race is America's longest running sporting event having started in 1874. A yearly event, which always brings the cream of celebrities, and the world's one percenters to the race ground. They come to wear their best clothes and hats and to be seen, and to be in front of any TV camera. Behind the scenes it is one week of excess, drinking, drugs, and out in the open sex as far as your eyes could see.

Horses came in from all over the world, and I always worked on those horse charters. These were million dollars plus animals, nothing but the best for them. Their owners always paid bonuses to us to ensure their animal was given extra special treatment. Most often it was cash but clothes, cocaine and lots of sex were offered up by these stupidly rich people.

The same thing happened again in November, when Lexington's Keeneland world famous horse auction occurs. This annual event is where some of the world's best breeding stock can be bought. Again, many of the world's 1%ters like the Queen of England, rich Arab Sheiks. Oil rich, pretend cowboys from Texas and Oklahoma came to spend some of their money. Breeders and horse mavens from around the world always showed up and mingled. Bill Murry and William Shatner, both had horse ranches, were always there. The other people who were always there would be mobsters. The horse business was used by the Mafia to clean money. Buy a horse at Keeneland then keep it for a period. After a while they would sell those investments, more offended to another Mafia guy. These guys would just keep flipping the horse moving the price up, or value up after each sale.

It is after the sale when these people really let loose. Again, lots of alcohol, sex and open serious drug use being the standard behavior year after year.

I got to meet a lot of jockeys like Pat Day through my mother, who had met many riders through her times in rehab and then AA. It seems racing a horse, at breakneck speed, squeezing every ounce of effort out of your ride can cause extreme stress. They like their horses cannot take drugs, so alcohol was the answer.

Where there is a racehorse, there can be found lots of steroids and injection pain meds like Nubian. So even before these plan loads of animals arrived. We always knew these products would also be found and would not be hard to sell. I love these two events every year and even now when May and the Derby comes around, I get home sick of those good old days knowing exactly what is actually really happening behind the scenes.

Chapter 11

New Additions to My Life

The summer of 1989 In Memphis I won first place in the Best Body of Memphis. I had been flown to MEM to live and train with Tommy and Terri Gollahon of Golds Gym in Germantown/ Memphis Tennessee.

What I do remember most was thar MEM was the most racist town I've ever been to, and I grew up in the deep south. It is the white part of town, and they did not like outsiders. A cop told me one day. "We killed Martin Luther King here boy, and don't you forget it." He was so proud as if he himself had pulled the trigger. Too bad times do not heal blackened hearts of ignorance.

The competition was held at a bar on Beale Street, the place was called MADISON AVENUE. The prize was a nice chunk of cash, plus I met a local News Reporter, a beautiful Swedish blond, who made the rest of my stay in town quite memorable.

On the trip home I sat next to Rudy Guiliani, quite a different man than the disgraced person he would become. He had successfully prosecuted lots of New York mobsters including John Gotti just a few years earlier. We talked about how important the immigration of Germans and Italians were to the success of the United States and its most successful growth.

November 7th, 1989, the Berlin wall came down in Germany and forty-eight hours later I was there. I met Langhammer's family members I had only heard of. I was also to find out part of the extended family lived in Argentina. My visit to east Germany was a real eye opener. Where West Germany grew and prospered after the war. No capital improvements were to be found in the East. It was like a walk back in time, pre-WW2. The communist way was never nourishing and with shortages of everything. Black markets were thriving, and several of my uncles and cousins were surviving by engaging in the sale of certain in demand items. Yet they all wanted me to bring them to America, "You are our Famous, Rich, Successful American Family, why not?" They were like us all wanting more than what we have, even if it was just a little bit better.

It was on this trip I found out the German I spoke; my family spoke, was what is call Swabian Dialect. Where most German speakers use high German or Hochdeutsche Mundarten. Think of someone from Harvard speaking English and then someone from Texas Tech speaking English. Do **you-all** understand? Yeah well, I did learn to speak, the proper High German. Work too only wanted me to speak only high German. "None of that Tex-sun/German, "as my boss called it.

I met Lisa Jo in 1989. She was a flight attendant from one of my flights I was working on unloading. She took one look at me and knew she had to have me, she thought she had hit the mother lode. Muscles, handsome, muscles, good stable job, did I mention muscles. She was definitely a muscle lover. She was a classic beauty, trapped in a killer body, which she loved to use in bed. Nothing was off limits to her. Top all that off with such a charming personality. Lisa was twenty-eight years-old and though I was only twenty-four, I knew I had finally found my soul mate.

1990 found me busy shooting a national TV commercial for American Airlines, my employer. It was shot in San Francisco and the commercial ran at that year's Super Bowl. The Superdome in New Orleans. The game was totally one sided. The 49'ers 55 // The Broncos 10. For a few years I would receive residuals every time the ad showed on TV.

In August of 1991 my first child was born, Dasch. It turned out to be a bittersweet event. I was now a father to a big baby boy. Unfortunately, he came in a package deal with his mother. I found out way too late about Lisa Jo. First, she was bi-polar, and actually had three distinct different personalities. She went from one personality character to another, and I never knew who or what I would be facing when I came home. At least one of her personalities was very mean spirited and vindictive. Another one of her personally was just a crazy irrational thinking person. When that one came out you never could tell what crazy things she would say or crazy action she might take. The third one, which was her work personality. Which was very manipulative, though she could be quite charming when she wanted to get something.

In many cases it was just to make sure my life was miserable as possible. Example being, Lisa Jo lied to the courts system claiming I was abusive to her and Dasch.

The Dallas County 330th family Court made me attend a psychiatric evaluation, not her. I was only given one visit a week with my boy and then only under supervision at Dallas's counties Family Connection Center.

I did eventually get full custody of Gunther. I was educated and had an excellent job, and they could not find anyone to collaborate with Lisa's domestic abuse claims.

Lisa Jo on the other hand, she was an alcoholic, psycho.

The real kicker came when she did the unthinkable. Lisa Jo crossed the union picked line in 1993. Durning her Unions Strike. Unions have long memories, and their influence reaches into lots of areas you would never have thought they could. This case being one of them. She got fired.

Robin Williams uses to say." God gave man two brains, one between his ears, the other between his legs. Unfortunately, the manufacturer only provided enough blood to operate one at a time."

I wish I had considered that information before I had met Lisa-Jo. It would be something I did think about from that point on regarding relationships.

Before Lisa Jo, I had a tough time opening up to a woman to show them the real Russell Langhammer. After this relationship, it would be even more difficult. I hurt and feared that no-one would ever love me if they knew my past and who I really was.

The old wall came down and Rusty the narcissist was back. Out on the make, anywhere anytime.

In the early 90's I became close with a few Texas Rangers baseball players. I was helping them work out in the gym for off-season training. There I met Bobby Witt and through him I met Kari, his sister. She and I dated for almost a year. It opened me to the inside lifestyle of baseball players. My friendship with Bobby ended when she and I broke up. What I found out while I was inside and partying with these athletes. They were nothing like football players, or body builders. They screwed each other's wives, just as a challenge. They jacked with each other's careers and spoke trash behind each other's backs. They as a group were disgusting and I lost all my respect for baseball players in general. I was glad back in my school days I chose track and football over baseball.

Then my luck changed, I was to meet Melissa, a German born gymnast in 1998. After being introduced to her by an old friend. She and her family were living in Kansas City. My German accent she found amusing. She was 23 young and beautiful. Raised in the old European way and we married in 1999 in a Catholic church. All her and all of my German family on both sides came as well. It was an immense success, and it may have been one of the happiest times in my life.

She wanted a family right away and thought bringing Dasch into our family to live a normal life would be a good start. Lots of money was spent, until finally the court gave us custody.

Lisa Jo then took Dasch and ran to Mexico. I would not see him again until he was eighteen. By then Lisa Jo had done a real number on him. Creating a mean spirted, racist hate filled young man. Even today I cannot be in the same room with him for very long. It breaks my heart.

Chapter 12

New Beginnings and An Ending

August 25, 1999, started a little differently. First, I had taken part of the day off in order to go to an eight-year-old's birthday lunch with my son. I had gotten back in time to unload 757 belly and to prepare the plane for an outbound MIA Miami trip. When I opened the back belly of the aircraft I saw a sea of AR-15 barrels pointing directly at me. They were DEA and they were taking over my gate. It was called the Organized Ramp Rats Bust. Almost 60 people were to be arrested nationwide. It had been a two- and half-year investigation that also included New York, Philadelphia, Baltimore, Miami. They picked up freight handlers, ramp agents, sky chefs and service workers. A Federal Inspector of Immigration and one from Naturalization and another one from the Department of Agricultural inspector, were all arrested that day.

The Chicago Mob ran our union, and they sent me a pointed message when I first joined up. **NO POWDERs, zip.**

A guy by the name of Eddie Garcia had a job similar to mine. He and his crew got caught with the Mobs cocaine. They were all tried and convicted. Then somehow all died on their ride to prison. Another couple of Miami workers were caught selling coke by union management. Both bodies were found floating in the Miami River. These messages were sent to members of the union and anyone who deals with stolen mob property.

I carried on and helped ship lots of cannabis and hash over the years. Never a single ounce of any powder. I was not arrested that day or any other day ever, for anything but fighting.

October 9 th 1999 at age 52 Darlene Huesmann Langhammer Stinson, of Bowling Green Ky, died of a broken heart. That is not what is written on my mom's death certificate. It says Arrhythmia failure.

I had spoken to her just an hour earlier. She had been waiting for my call, I guess, so, she would be able to get off her chest the burden she most certainly had been carrying way too long, for much of her life.

"Russell my son, I am sorry I was not the best mother you deserved. I made too many poor choices which affected you and our poor Ricky. Please forgive me Russell, please". I let her know I understood and told her she owed us nothing and we knew she had done her best. My mom was only looking for safety, love, acceptance.

"Remember our dance nights Russ? They were so much fun, won't they?" she asked, Time back then was so much simpler.

"I sure do mom, yeah, they were fun." I replied thinking back to those late nights with her.

When I was 12 years old, I had a mustache, and looked much older than my years. If mom wanted to go out dancing and could not get one of her friends to join her, I was recruited. No one ever asked me for an ID, we just walked in, found a spot to leave our coats, and then spent hours dancing. She would just let loose, bump and grinding all over the floor, and even on to me.

I think she had me there to keep the losers off her. We would get back home early in the morning, and if it was a school night. I had to go to school with very little sleep.

She ended up dying, at home in her sleep. She finally got the peace she spent her life looking for. Alcohol, and any drug that she could find and that would help dull her painful memories. Ones that would help her get through just one more day. It was to be her way out.

Mom had indeed made too many bad choices and it affected our lives. She would work hard when she was sober. Sometimes two jobs at once. She would work herself up in the company where she worked, but then she would end up having an affair with someone in management and fall off the wagon. Too many nights I would hear her come in with some guy. Years later, I would get a call from her crying, she had awoken up in some city and had no idea how or why. I would have to arrange for a cab to pick her up and take her to the nearest major airport and use my employee connections to fly her home. Over the years she found herself even imprisoned in Kentucky State Hospital in Lagrange Kentucky, the only law she broke was trying to kill herself four separate times. The state locked her up for her own safety.

Her worst memories as a child were the concentration camps in Germany during the war, in which she, her mother and uncle were forced to exist in for over a year. She would stay clean for years then one day fall off the wagon. She died of a broken heart I am sure of that.

Melissa got pregnant and gave birth on January 28th of 2003 to our son, Gunther, our miracle child. We had been trying to get pregnant for years. My poor wife had endured three previous pregnancies over the first few years of our marriage only to lose each one. Gunther was to be our last try. Success at last and he was so perfect.

Unexpected problems started right after Gunther's birth. Melissa changed. It probably was post-partum after birth depression. My opinion it was something no one knew much about at the time. I had hoped she would grow out of it. She rejected Gunther and me, wanting nothing to do with either of us. I put up with her attitude which put me through pure hell for Gunther's sake.

My life in photos

My father at age 8

Pop age ten.

My Grandfather Langhammer.

Grampa and Grandmother Pragtorw.

**Three generations of Langhammer's.
Dad, Me, & Opa**

The Langhammer's wedding Day.

My first Christmas with Mom, 1965.

Me and my father 1966.

My dad at work

Me, Santa, and Ricky 1970.

Blue, Mom, Me, Ricky, and Randy, summer of 1970

Me age 6

Where there is water, I will be found.

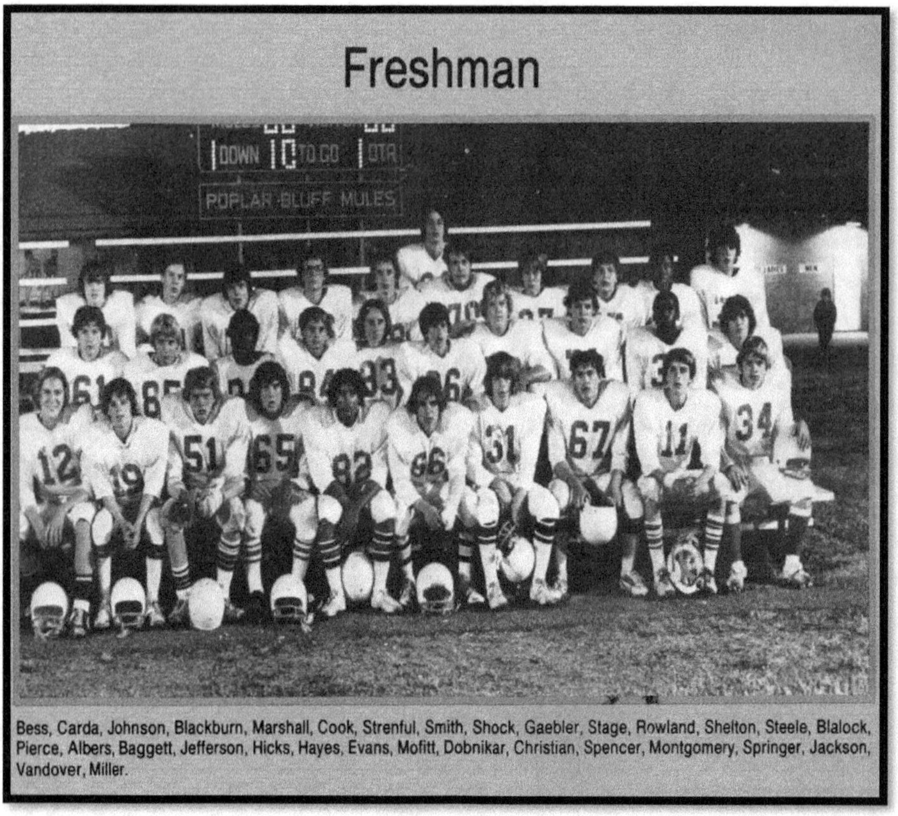
Freshman
DOWN
TO GO
QTR
POPLAR BLUFF MULES
Bess, Carda, Johnson, Blackburn, Marshall, Cook, Strenful, Smith, Shock, Gaebler, Stage, Rowland, Shelton, Steele, Blalock, Pierce, Albers, Baggett, Jefferson, Hicks, Hayes, Evans, Mofitt, Dobnikar, Christian, Spencer, Montgomery, Springer, Jackson, Vandover, Miller.

My first football team.

SPORTS SHACK

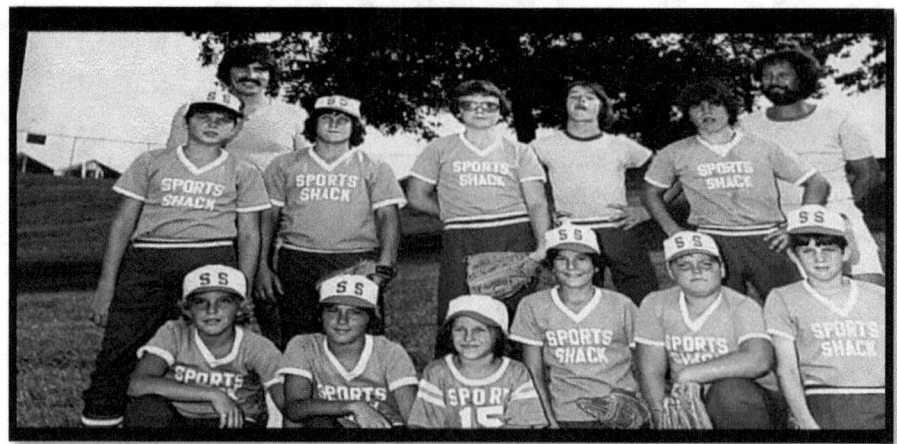

My first baseball team.

My favorite was running hurdles. State Chamion 1982 and 1983.

Yeah, I am winning.

Flying over the wood.

Being serious.

Voted senior year: Two Most Flirtatious in the class of 1983.

College Student

Male stripper @ Toy Tiger

Living the dream.

My Cover Boy Look.

Hanging with my teammates.

Yea, I got the ball.

My dream came true, I made it I am a Dallas Cowboy.

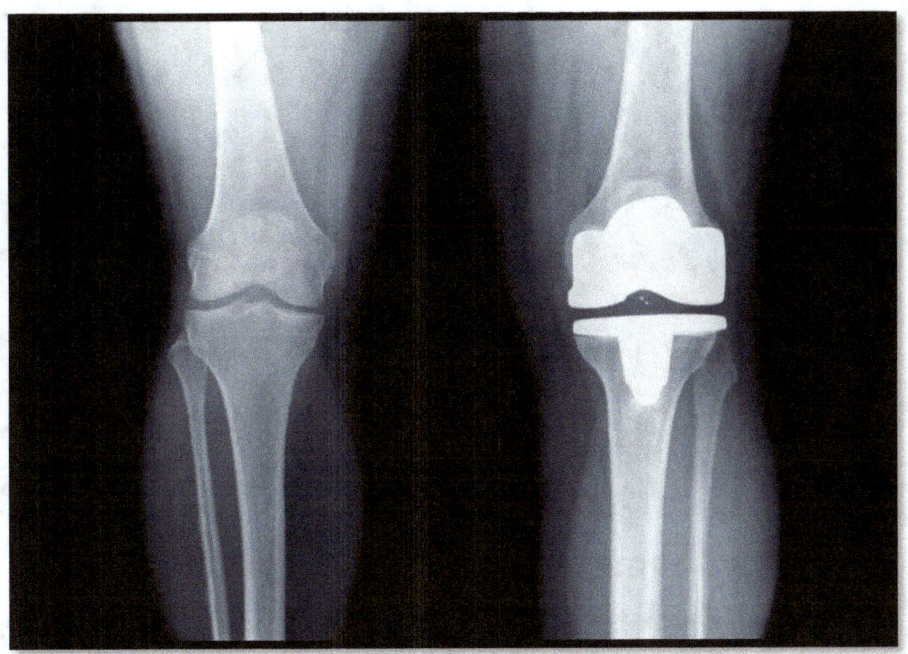

My knees were under contract.

Gunther's first dog, Baby.

Gunther reading the funny papers with me.

Me and Gunther, after my first pacemaker.

Celsa and Gunther

Proud Poppa.

Hard at work planning the layout of the load, old school before computers.

A Cup-pa Joe.

Another workday on the hot concrete, 1970.

My first body building competitions.

Look I made a muscle.

Texas power Lifting Champion @ 242 Pounds in 1993.

The wait before weighing in.

I got my pro-card.

The young Branch Warren on the left.

The future, the present, the past.

And a one and a two.

Me and Ronnie Coleman

Third place win for me, Ronnie Coleman won first place.

My magazine cover boy look, 1993.

In my prime

One open heart surgery, and four pacemakers later, I am still working out.

Yes, I do have Blue eyes.

You're looking at what should be a Dead Man summer of 2012.

Living a great life.

Fish on.

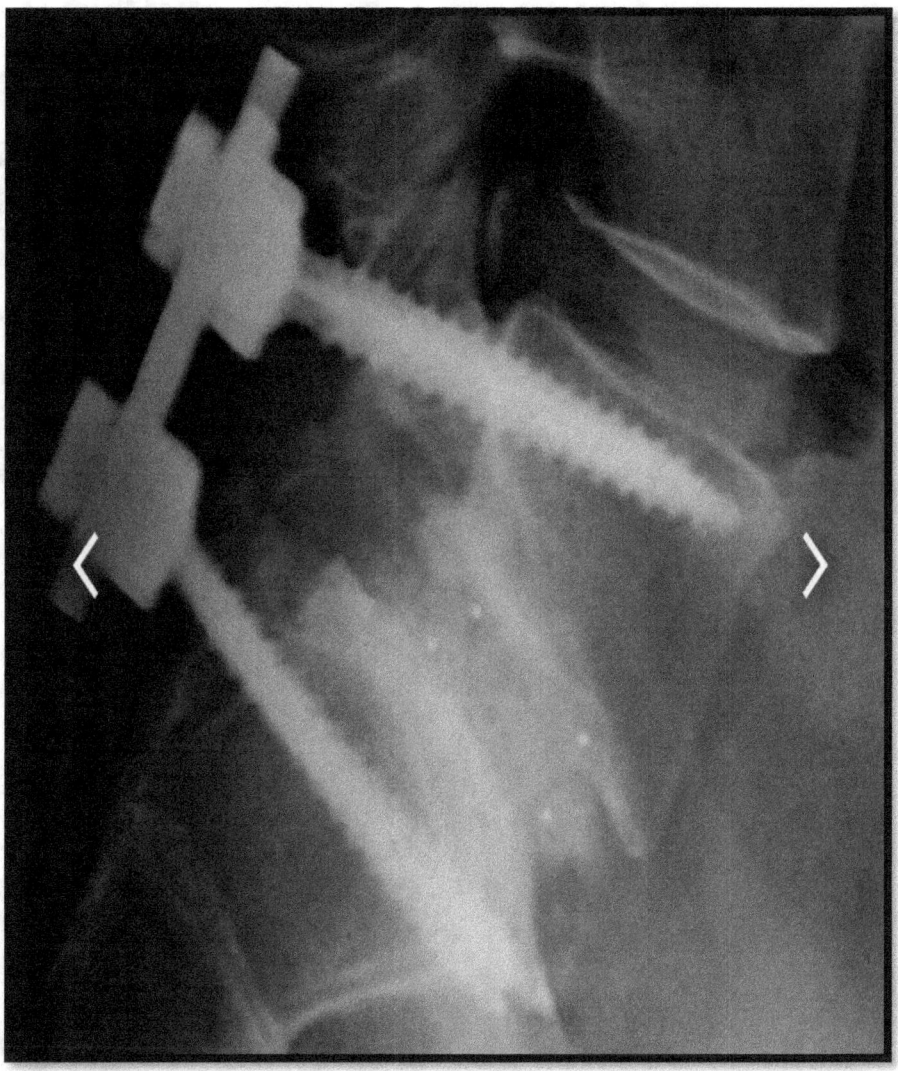

The winter storm of 2000 caused me to fall off a 20' tall scaffold, resulting in sever head and back injuries while working at DFW airport.

Over the years they have become regular visitors to my house for me.

So thankful to still be here.

PAIN IS MY COMPANION

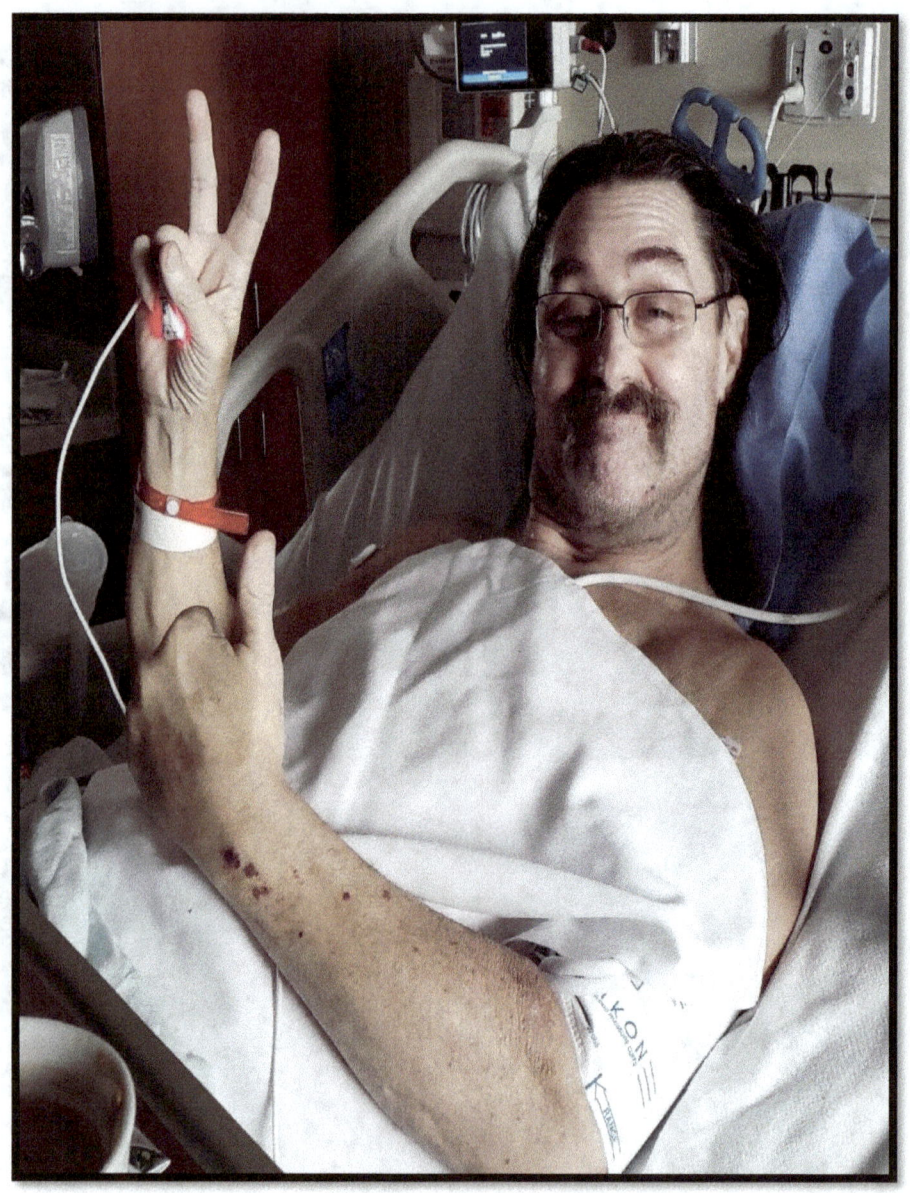

Back here again.

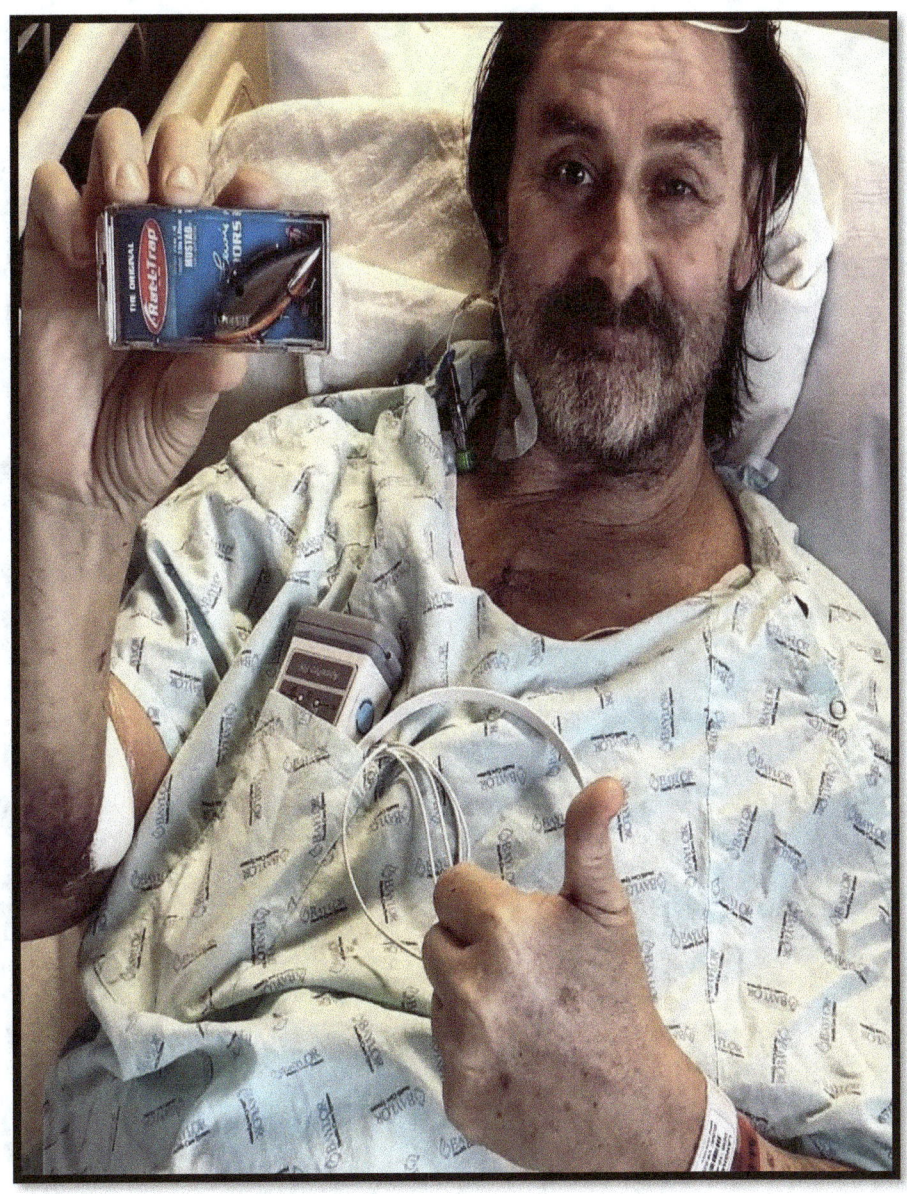

I want to try this one out soon.

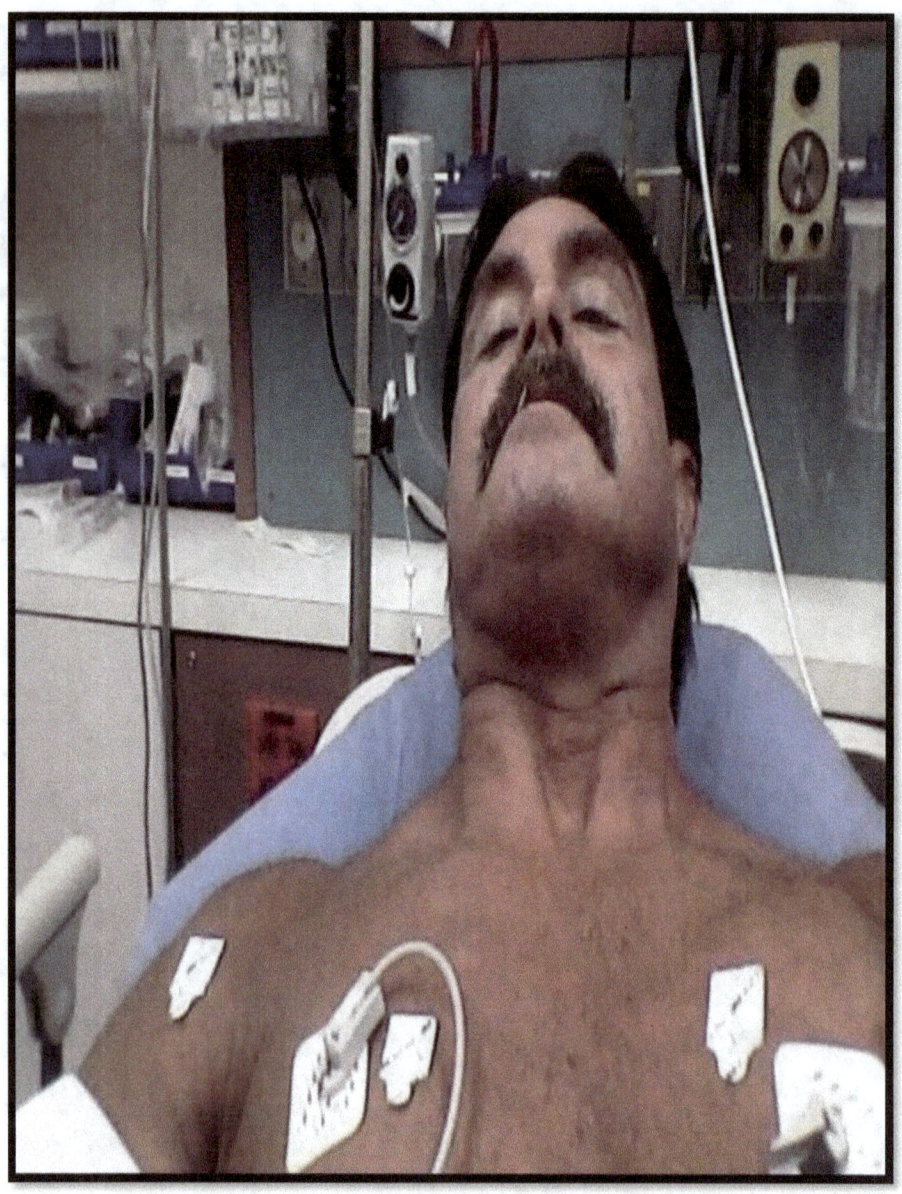

Not a typical commercial for Toothpicks.

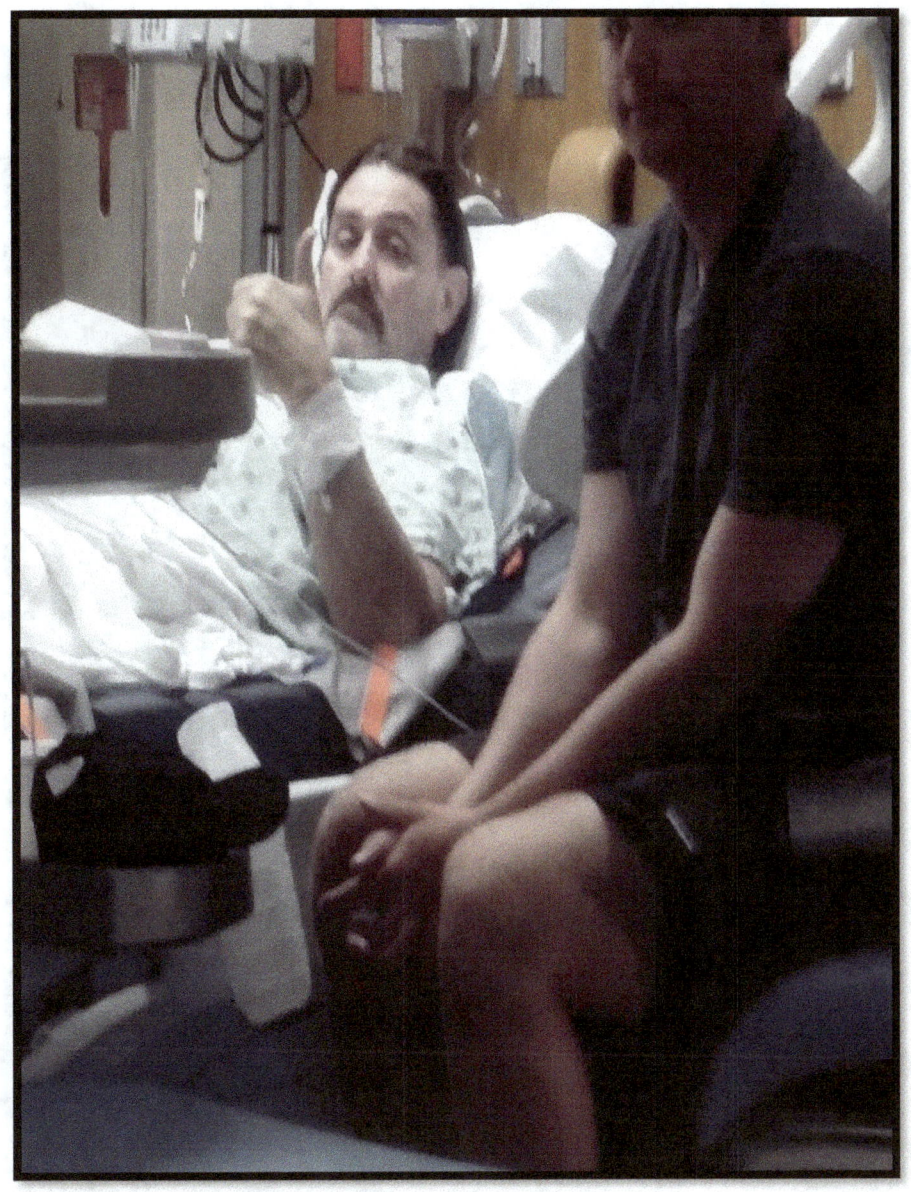

Gunther keeping me company.

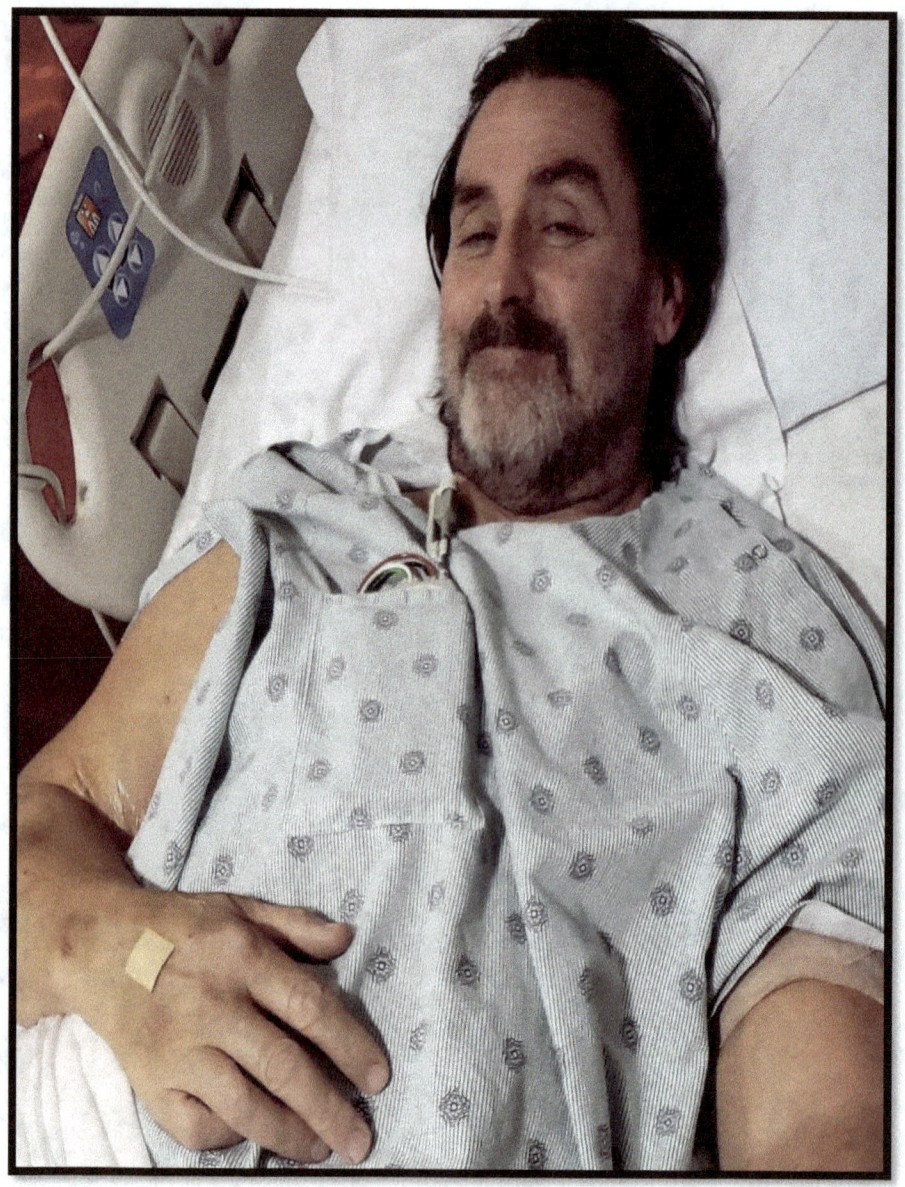

I am still alive. Still fighting for life.

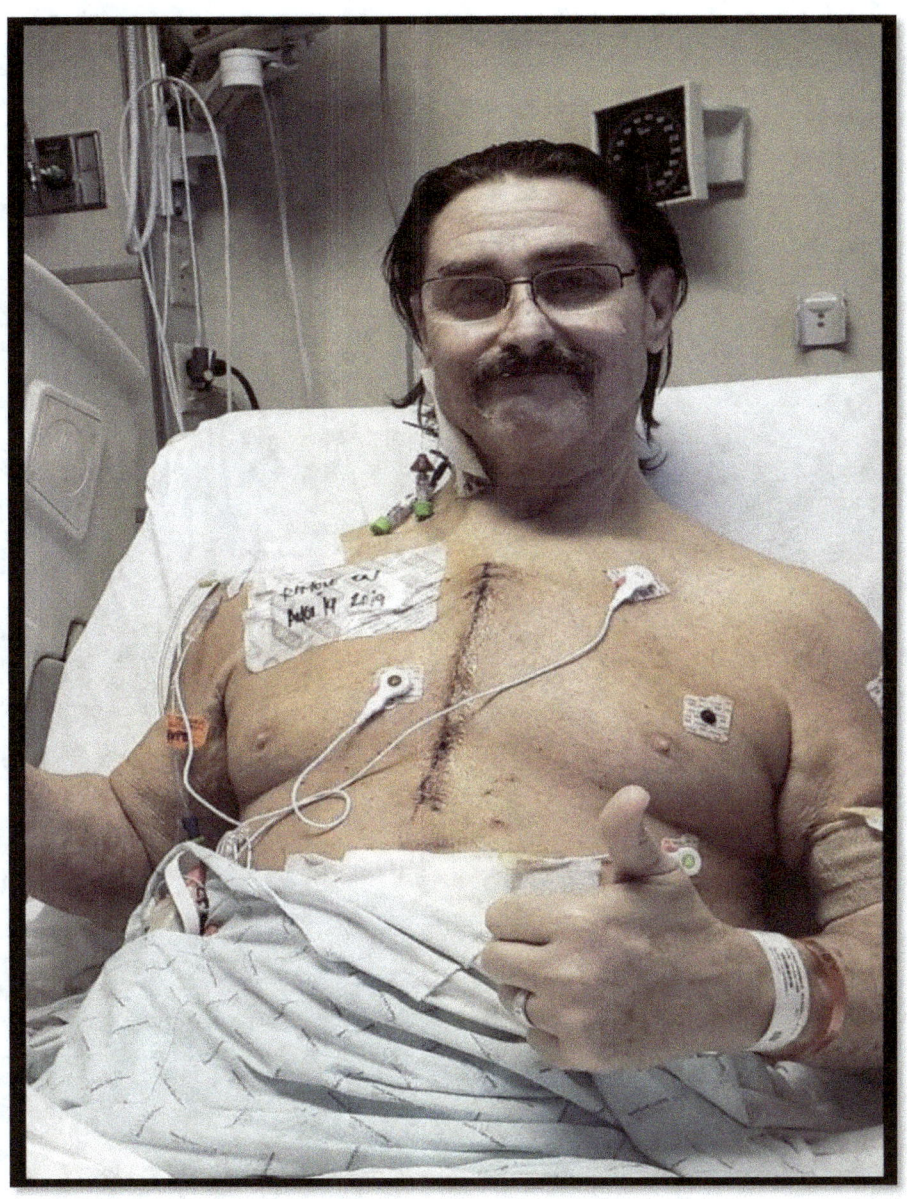

After Open Heart Surgery.

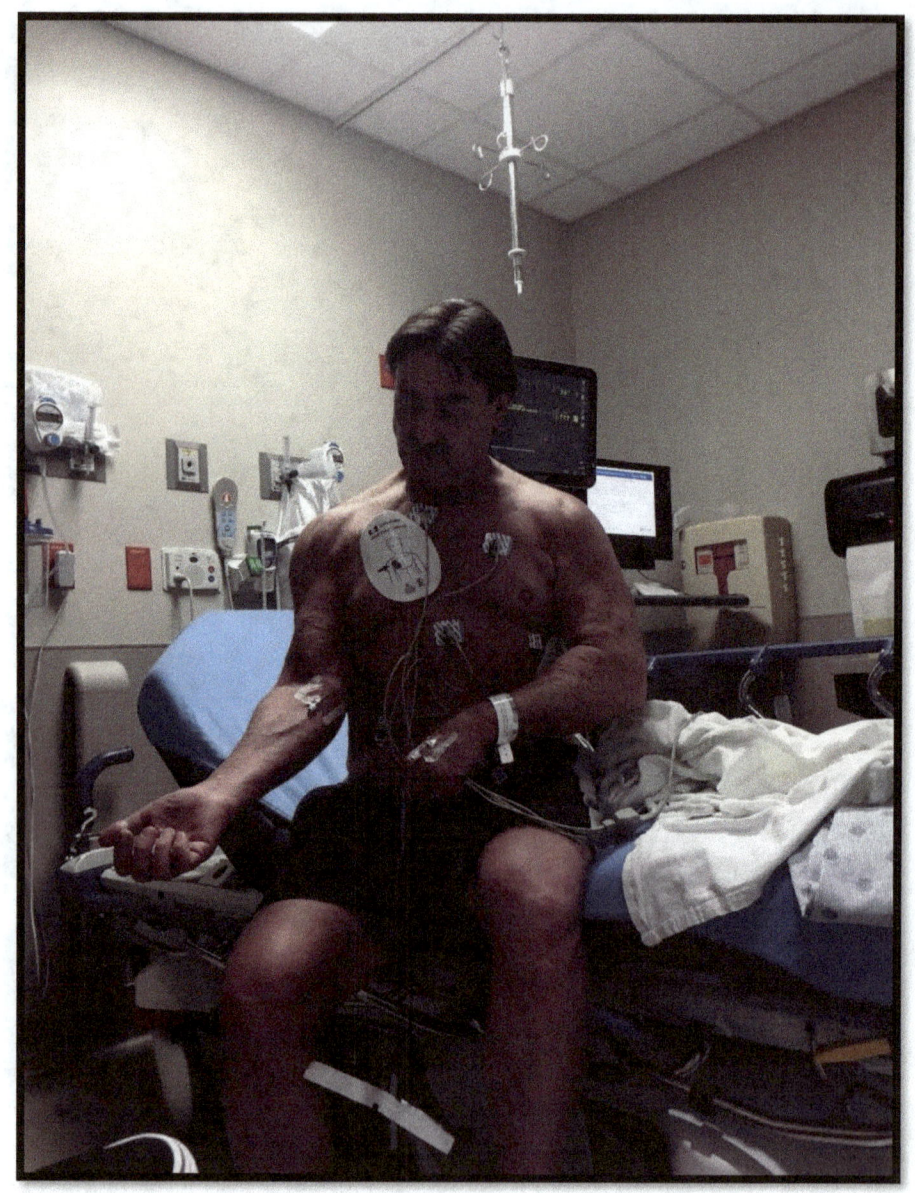

Which wire goes where?

Gunther supporting his pop.

A Familiar Face

Guess Who?
Kerry Von Erich

Competing.

Another wonderful day.

Dam this is heavy.

PAIN IS MY COMPANION

We're showing muscles.

Gerrrrr!

PAIN IS MY COMPANION

Any kind of publicity is good.

Just confirming what I have been saying all along.

November 7th, 1989, Berlin Wall Falls. November 9th I was here celebrating freedom for my East German Family.

My lady makes me happy. Sharing life's journey.

A lake date.

Sharing time in nature.

Still in love.

Outside the Old Eohany Street Synagogue in Budda.

Handsome Couple

Happy Wife Happy Life.

Showing more muscles.

Grand Kids.

Grand kids.

My favorite flower

Working in the garden

Looking good for a dead man.

Daddy's Girls

Wake n Baking.

Chapter 13

Dangerous Work

Airports are 24/7 construction sites behind the scenes. Lots of large pieces of equipment like moving conveyor belts. Heavy motorized tugs move airplanes out of bays, and pull trailers loaded with freight and luggage to and frow. Super duty Taylor forklifts with six-foot-tall tires and 40,000 pounds of lifting capacity moving large jet engines to and back from the repair shop.

One afternoon a friend of mine, Carol, was coming back from lunch and was not being very attentive when a Taylor carrying a 747 turbo-engine did not see her and ran her over. I watched and could do nothing but scream as I saw her explode in front of my eyes. Within minutes UPS had attorney's and an ambulance on the ramp. Another day we were unloading a 727 and lightning hit the plane and all six of my crew had to go to the hospital for observation. My coworker Smitty's hair turned gray in patches. He was just touching the door while also holding on to a Cochran loader. He became the connector, the wire. All the electricity from the lightning ran through him as he became the ground. The Doctor told him it was a miracle he was still alive. Back injuries were occupational expectation, and loss fingers were a dime a dozen.

December 1st, 1994, I was working to help unload the LD-8 container into the plane's cargo hole. I threw the steel wire curtain on top One of the cargo hook's broke loose from curtain and, as it sprung free, I was lucky it just missed my face, which would have killed me if it had hit me. Yes, it missed my head but caught my ear and it tore it off and all the flesh around it, away from my head. I had to have, two operations to sew the flesh back on, and one to re-create the ear. I have lived through lots of painful things in my life, but as I look back that was one of the most painful things I have ever experienced, plus the sound of my flesh being pulled apart from my head, will never leave my psyche. I have also gotten run over by a forklift and had to have knee surgery again in the 1990's. I had two more work-related surgeries. Doctors prescribed tons of opiate and benzodiazepines along with Celebrex and Viox so I could work. The last two have since been pulled from the market due to the side effects they have on the patients' hearts.

November 11, 2000, was a day filled with one disaster after another. Today I would have just said it started as a cluster, F//. A front came in from the North Hill country, bringing three to six inches of freezing rain and sleet into the metroplex. Followed by another three inches of snow on top of that. DFW airport was backed up with a few of last night's arrivals then the mornings too. Plus, the ones that had been diverted. I had been working non-stop for way too many hours. Then just as I was ready to leave a rouge plane pulled in. The fight had been on our runway sitting for over six hours waiting to get orders to take off. The passengers were going crazy, so the pilot, who was a friend of mine and knew I was working, without any advanced noticed pulled out of line and crossed over runways and wants me to guide him into my bay. I should have known better. I was dead tired, but I pulled over the twenty-foot-tall maintenance stand so the pilot could see me and my hand signals. It was a very tight fit as it was. No room for error. He followed my directions to a T.

As I was about to turn and retreat. A gust of wind hit me exactly right and the steps were covered with snow on top of wet ice. I fell backwards landing on my back and head. I broke my L4/ L5/ and S1 in my back. My skull was broken, and my brain began swelling I had to have a Gallaudet and Morph done. I woke up in the hospital only speaking German. My wife and brother were there and translated information back and forth to the Doctors and staff. I would watch some TV show and could not understand what they were saying. It took four days before my brain shrank back and I begin recognizing English words and began speaking English again. To the joy of all my family.

It was at this point in my life, I had opiates reintroduced in my life.

I had lived most of my thirty-five years of life without painkillers. I had lived with all kinds of pain all my life. At times I had even enjoyed it, at least when it stopped hurting. Most people feel intense pain in the beginning. At the point and time, it hurts less to a various degree, then at some point it stops getting worse and actually starts feeling better. I lived thirty-five years with that type of pain. What I was feeling now was a brain on fire and throbbing continually. Cradling my brain, is my fractured skull and face. Creating its own dance of different pain all over my head and face. Even my hair hurt. If things are not already bad enough, I cannot walk, my back looks like pieces from a jigsaw puzzle and it too has its own set of pains. I could not sleep; I was in nine different pains, not any good ones. All =constant hurt. Since I could not kill myself, I took the drugs they supplied. Thinking I can beat this shit when I get back to my old self. Sure, I am Russell Langhammer after all. Nothing is impossible.

I was back to work in four months, not 100% but there every day. Mellissa was pregnant at the time and no money is coming in. I had no choice but to work and still needed the opioids to get through another day. Promising myself as soon as….

September 11th, 2001, Melissa and I were in Cabo for a week and were getting ready to head back to the airport to come home. We watched on our TV set in horror as the American Airlines jets hit one of the twin towers. I knew that pilot and crew. I am thinking to myself." WTF, is going on here there must be more to this." Then again it happened we knew this was not some accident., but who? We sat in front of the TV the entire day. The whole town was silent. Open but only TV or radio news was being played. People spoke in whispers as if speaking out would disturb the dead people's souls. It would be three days before we would be able to get home. I knew crew personnel on two of those crashing flights. The morale back at Dallas/Ft. Worth airport, especially at my work, was not exactly high. The airport was still busy, but it seemed to me to have a different feel to it.

On Thanksgiving Day 2001 I was working and got struck squarely in the face by a Steel Samsonite, it did nothing to the luggage, but my nose was squashed across my face, I had to have surgery again to fix the Deviated Septum. While in the surgery they took out my adenoids and tonsils too. Then sent me home with my pain killers. No sooner than I had got home than I started bleeding out. My wife had to drive me back to the emergency room, where they saved my life. I was in a coma for three days and was lucky to have survived the CELEBREX and VIOXX poisoning.

I learned that even well-trained medical people can be lazy, or stupid. I am much more aware these days as to what prescription drugs I put in my body and how they interact with what else I am using in my body. Sometimes a simple vitamin XYZ might have a strange effect when combined with an ABC drug. Something as common as Grapefruit voids out certain medications. I have had to educate myself, to stay safe.

Melissa dumped me in 2005. She said she could not handle any more surgeries or pharmaceuticals. She left, then filed for bankruptcy. Leaving me responsible for all our unpaid bills.

She did not, though, restrict my time with my son. My relationship with Gunther has always been solid and he brings me so much pleasure to see the way he has become a great human being.

Chapter 14

I See a Bright Future

At work, I met a lovely person who was to become my best friend. Celsa Gallegos/Dominguez, she was from Mexico and her family too were Jewish, though not practicing ones. She helped me in the early days with Gunther.

As best friends we go fishing sometimes, on our days off. I would tell her about of the different women I was going out with, just like she was a male friend. She got to see that side of me and never passed judgment. Then one day on the lake, I was telling her, "Celsa, I feel so dirty, so hollow, I am so unhappy."

She looked up to me and her face broke out in a smile. It seemed to start on one side of her face and go all the way across to the other side. White pearls flashing at me. "Hammer, I love you, didn't you know that. I have been waiting for you to see. For you to stop chasing smoke. Have you?"

I must be honest; I ran like crazy. I continued my old ways. Then one day I finally realized I missed my best friend. Celsa had seen something good in me, even I could not see. She loved me not for my body, or my fame. She knew my worst and still loved me. It was to be not just another blessing in my life. This time I had my eyes open. I brought flowers, accompanied by an apology. It took a while, she had to be convinced I was sincere and wanting a life with only her.

We moved in together in 2008. For once in my life everything is running smoothly and crisis free.

Then in the early morning hours in February of 2009, I woke up in such pain. I was crying and did not realize it, and I had trouble swallowing. A fire was in my throat, I thought I had swallowed a burning meatball.

It proved to be cancer of my mouth and jaw. The Doctor said probably from too many years of chewing tobacco. I had my lower jaw on one side removed during Mayella Facial surgery. Followed by nine weeks of chemotherapy. Which turned out, destroyed my heart, while killing the Cancer.

October of the same year 2009 I got my first pacemaker; I was only 44 years old.

January 2010 I finally felt alive again and began to work out using coach Kingery regiment from my high school days. "When lost, you can always find the self you want to be Russell, in the gym." His voice would sing in my head.

November of 2012 my first-place makers wires burst through my skin, causing another emergency surgery. I am in screaming out loud pain and I am thinking, is this ordeal ever going to end.

I have had only a few men who have impressed me, but one that I have to put on top of my list was the greatest showman of all time. He put it all on the line every time he performed. Evil Knievel. No smoke and mirrors, no hidden key or pick in his mouth. It was him against fear, death and more often than not some pain if he miscalculated. Just one sneeze in mid-flight a sudden puff of wind, or an insect or bird encounter midair that could not be planned for, and he would land with only leather and a plastic helmet for protection. I can remember as a nine-year-old sitting in front of the TV waiting for the big jump. I am thinking to myself, what kind of crazy courage he must have taken to strap himself into the skyrocket cycle and be shot up in the air over a huge cliff to try to fly over the snake river and land on the other side of the canyon. Who else would ride/ fly a rocketed motorcycle? Throughout my worst times, I could always remember back to my hero and know it can be done.

Chapter 15

Decision Time

From November 2000 when I had my fall at work Until October 31, 2015, I was a drug addict. Not a day would go by without me taking something to kill the pain and the huge amount of anger I was carrying around. I blamed everything and everybody. I was called, *the Ramp Nazi* and ran ruff shot over my fiefdom. I used it as an excuse instead of facing the problem head on like I was used to doing. I had begun hating myself. I knew I was a liar, a cheater, a bully, and totally out of control SOB. I would run into people after my rehab who told me of things, I had said to them or some petty action that had made me crazy and my response to that situation. People I had known years later told me I was hated. I remember none of these incidents that I was confronted with later. All I could do was to ask them to forgive me for the injurious behavior. Some did others just blew me off, understandable too.

I finally made the choice to get help after losing my family, my job, and the ability to compete.

2015 I entered Valley Hope a rehab center voluntarily. I was to check in November first, 2015. Staying until December 31, just before New Year. "I can do this," I say to myself. The facility was very nice on the outside. Inside was just what you would expect of a rehab hospital. White or light green walls Lots of identical small rooms with one bed, a mini-closet, one bedside table with a non-descript lamp. In the drawer of course was a Gideon bible, plus one dresser. Lastly the one uncomfortable chair. The bathroom was so small I had to put my feet into the shower to sit on the commode.

There were a few communal areas and a small library. Several meeting rooms for group therapy meetings and a few single one on one rooms for each of the therapists that they used as their offices. We all ate in a small cafeteria or in our rooms. The staff was mostly made up of young therapist, just out of college, first job dealing with crazy people and drug addicts. Add the nurses along with their bruiser aids and you have most of the personnel I delt with on a day-to-day basis. Lastly, they had a doctor on staff to write the meds they used in their treatment. What a scam these people were running. The prices were out of the world for a little talking therapy, lots of filling foods, and new drugs to help get you through withdrawals. One addiction for another one. "This is Bull Shit" I told them. I came to get clean, not looking for a substitute. The drug of the day was Suboxone, they forced me to take it in order to stay. Go, stay, they did not care they already got paid for the two months with or without me. This drug would not allow me to sleep, not during the day or night. Twelve days in, and I had not one moment of sleep. I am getting more pissed and aggressive every day. My heart began acting up without sleep. The Clinics DR..X was from India, and I was to find out latter, he had lost his license and was not legally able to write prescriptions for the rehab Center but did. On day twelve He transferred me to a place called Spring Wood A rehab Center for heart and lung patients.

I came out just a little bit better than when I went in. Yes, I was free of opiates but not free from my old companion, **Mr. Pain.**

Chapter 16

Clean

Whenever I find myself having to restart my life, I can find comfort in the old and familiar. Two things Coach Kingery gave me so many years ago. The truth we all must face, he would simply say." This is life win or lose you got to face it." And a place to find myself would be through the regiment in the gym. Free weights, Dumbbells, and the Universal Weight Machine. Three days a week. Of course, I had to start slowly in the beginning, and stop myself from over doing it. Yet, I was still pushing myself. It might even have been the familiarity of the pain I knew would come. Somehow even that had some comforting benefits. Psychologically for sure. As you might expect, I am not the type of person when they run into life's problems get unhinged. Needing to see someone to discuss it. That approach may work for some people, but it is not for me. If there is one thing anyone who knows me will say. Russell tells things the way he sees it. Truthfully. When I come to those times in my own life, I will open up the issue. View through my eyes experience and call myself out if needed. Coming back from death has given me a fresh prospective and appreciation for each day and I realized, Russell no longer has time for Bull Shit.

Chapter 17

And Then

I was weaning off Benzos and was having trouble sleeping, everything around me seemed to be closing in so at the beginning of October 2017 I got my doctor to give me something to help. The medication they gave me had a side effect when added to the Celebrex and Vioxx I was already on. I went into a coma. Not the type where I passed out, no I just fell into a deep sleep. Not for a few hours or a day, but like everything I do it had to be bigger than everyone else. I was out for nine days as if my body was possessed. I remember nothing of those lost days. I was told later I was violent, both verbally screaming, my physical anger level was uncontrollable. I was put in a strait jacket so as not to hurt myself or and one else. On the ninth day I woke up in a padded room, Celsa was feeding me soup. Two guards were also in the room, and another man who I did not recognize. "What in the hell is going on baby? Why am I tied up?" She smiled back at me, knowing I was finally back. I looked at the stranger and asked. "Who are you?"

"I am Dr…. your psychiatrist, do you know your name, who is this lady?"

I answered his questions. "Great you're not crazy, you must have had a bad reaction to the." I totally lost those nine days and had to learn from my family what I had been through. My wife, Celsa, was there every day feeding me and making sure there would be someone from the family to be there when I woke up. She has been my rock since we first met. A true blessing of mine along with our kids.

2018 I came out of the closet so to speak; the cannabises closet that is. I become more verbal as an activist for Cannabises reform.

In 2019 was my year to spend more time in the hospital than at my home. Starting with January where I made two appearances. I was in Austin for A legalization of Marijuana rally in February and found myself admitted to Dell Seaton hospital. March first I was back in the emergency room and when I awoke a Priest giving me last rights. Fooled him. April 8th and 21st. May June July all back again to adjust my pacemaker. I was shocked so many times my muscles were constantly sore, and my heart felt like fire and electricity pulling me in several different directions all at once during each of these procedures.

I'm half-way through the year and it does not look like it was going to get better. Thankfully my Celsa and our family kept me going, that and a ton of marijuana. I would not take narcotics, so I went back to mother nature. Cannabises saved my life.

August fourth in 2019 I awoke with a runaway heartbeat. The proper name is Super Ventricle Tachycardia. It was as if I had taken a full shot of pure adrenalin. At Melodist hospital they try shocking me to get the heart to go back in rhythm. I was screaming, cursing, throwing a fit. The head nurse came over and asked me to calm down and stop the cussing. On each side of her were two very large men. Mean time all the shocking did not stop the rapid heartbeat I was experiencing. In the end they ended up shocking me/ my heart sixty-four times to wear down my pacemaker's battery. Thus, my response back to the nurse was not particularly nice. My pain level was beyond ten, plus I know there were lots more coming and nothing I could do but scream and yell. One of the orderly's was trying to help me between shocks, when I was hit while he had a hand on me. The shock threw him across the room, so you can get an idea what each one of those 64 hits were like to me. Once they got the pacemaker's battery drained, I was then moved to Baylor Scott and White's Heart and Lung Center.

They opened me up. And began after opening my chest to do a heart catheter and five-way CABG bypass surgery and then received pacemaker number four. They had problems getting my rhythm correct so they did Ablation, but it did not work, so October I had another Ablation. Finally, after several more shock sessions I was back home and recuperating.

I have had to adjust to my life, to accommodate a daily download from Dallas Baylor hospital @ 10:30 every night. No matter where my body is in the world, I get zapped. I know it is coming and no matter how many times I go through it, I am never ready, and it is always worse than I expect. The wires that run under my skin and muscles are eight gage wires. Think barbed wire fencing wire thickness, of course without the barbs. It is meant to carry serious power. The shock is multi-level. My body contracts, and it puts major strain on all the connected tissue, my muscles are pressed to their extreme. Then there is the burning hot 8 gage wires heating everything around. When electricity goes into your body it must also exit it somewhere. Mine does by burning a hole in my skin as it explodes out my body. All skin has moisture, that moisture heated up cause burning as well. Sometime the downloads will put me down to my knees. Other times it will pull me out of my sleep and if I am in bed, I vibrate the whole bed. As much as I hate this part of my life, the truth is the pain reminds me I am still alive and that this is my cost to wake up on this side of the ground every morning.

Years later I was back into the same Methodist Hospital with one of the kids who had hurt themselves. The same head nurse I had been so mean, was there. She saw me and ran up to give me a big hug.

"Dar-lin, I am so glad you made it," she said as she was squeezing me. I apologize for having been so mean and cursing her out. "You were in pain baby, I understood. I still do not know how you took it all, my lord."

We both seemed to have been able to resolve our parts of a terrible night. I know, I left feeling better.

I'll tell you the **real truth** why I am still here and still alive today.

It is because first my doctors told me in 2019 to go home and to take care of whatever business I needed to do before I died. Then a priest came in behind him and gave me last rights, again. I said to myself, screw you both. I am not that type of person. I am Russell Langhammer, I compete and we Langhammer's do not quit. I will not walk away from this challenge, even if it is the biggest I have ever faced before, in my 54 years of living so far.

If I learned one thing in all my years in gyms across the world. If you have a body issue, somebody has a fix. I had to find a fix but not just a chemical one but ones that mother nature could provide.

I had already begun reading up on Yoga and breath control to help with pain while the uncontrollable force races through me. I had not reached any expertise but anything that potentially helped I was open to look-in to and try. So naturally it is India where I started my journey to find more about mother nature's cures for my many pains.

Old India text sings the praises of cannabis and it's healing qualities were used in many salves and potions. I found that as far back as 1000 BCE the Hindi used cannabis for a very effective pain reliever. It was common for women's monthly pains. Earaches, and even given to pregnant women during childbirth. The Hindi's make a holy drink called Bhang. The holy drinks main ingredient is made from cannabis plants leaves.

Bhang it is said, is a drink that will cleanse your sins. It will allow you to become mentally ready to be united with the great spirt, **Siva**.

I was open to trying anything and I sure needed some of that sin cleaning. AMEN

If I was about to start a new healthier lifestyle, then let's do it correctly. I can now see why this is such a popular drink in India.

My next deep research was of other ancient Asia treatments. Of course, acupuncture, which I had done several times while competing. Also, I was to find lots of potions that had some very interesting animal parts. But guess what one of many of their ingredients that keep showing back up over and over was? Mother earth's gift to mankind, Cannabises.

First, early man only hunted the cannabises plant for just her seeds. They were humans' perfect food mixtures. Proteins, Fats and Carbohydrates. Then man found when the stems were sunk in water, they get pliable and it could be made into a binding material, early rope. The females would process the stocks down even more to make many different useful cloths. The holy roots and flowers were the last part of this plant that early man used as medicine to cure himself mentally, and physically.

In 2800 BCE China's Emperor Shen, considered the father of Chinese medicine, wrote the first book of pharmacopoeia. In it he used the whole cannabis plant as a component for many of his treatments. Along with various mushrooms.

I also found out, surprisingly, mushrooms had wonderful medical qualities as well. They are used for curing bronchial lung issues, cancers, it is used to help open wounds to heal. When added to any other treatment program they enhance the total curative effect of that treatment. Then when I found out mushrooms booted immune systems, helped lung issues and fought cancer, I was in.

No matter where I looked in early civilizations Rome, Greece, Turkey, Israel, Africa, Afghanistan, the Vikings and most all the early tribes of Europe all used cannabis for pain relief. Mushrooms too, were often an ingredient in the medicine given.

One of the most interesting facts I uncovered by accident was that what the Jewish religion calls holy oil. Oil only used in anointing holy visitors to the Temple in Jerusalem, and the few high priest who worked there. This holy oil had cannabis oil as one of its main ingredients. The holy oil was also found in every Jewish house of Jewish worship. It is in the everlasting light which can be found hanging above their pulpit. It shows the spirit of G-D residing in his house, it also while the oil burns, gets the holy houses participants high. Making those who are shackling or praying as the body moves sways, have a very enlightened experience.

2021 got better Though it was an emotional year. I finally had come to terms with the fact I was never going to be Mr. Macheso, but I was finally able to start going back to the gym. Three days a week, which helped bring a bit of familiar normality back to my life. I still had lots of visits to this and that doctor and regular visits back to Baylor hospital for updates.

I was able though to visit Bueno Aires Argentina and I got to meet more of my Langhammer family there.

Chapter 18

The Famous and Infamous

I have many friends, and some would become famous, a few infamous, but each had some influence on my life. I also rubber elbows with many famous people while working in the airline industry.

Growing up as a kid in the early 70's in Poplar Bluff, I had a young play mate from down the road. She was my age with blond hair and deep blue eyes, her name was Robin. We were buds, out chasing lizards or splashing in the creek looking for tadpoles. When not in school, with our bikes no place was beyond limits. One day while out and too far from home, I found I had a full blader and so I stopped riding and went into the bushes to pee. I looked over to my right and there she was next to me. She had dropped her shorts and squatted down to relieve herself too. Except for my mom and grand mom, we did not have a lot of men in our life at that time. She did not have a penis. "What happened to your penis?" I asked totally confused.

"Girls don't have Penis's silly; don't you know that?"

"No" I replied. I must have had a really dumb look on my face.

My first hands-on lesson on boy girl differences.

"Ok, I'll show you mine, then you show me yours."

My first sexual exposure, I liked it, something very naughty that made it exciting.

I tried the same approach to another girl in the neighborhood who I liked. Julie though, she did not fall for my innocence. We though did date later on becoming boyfriend and girlfriend in Junior High School. That was at least until Julie's family moved to the Dallas area. She would become a photo model. Then, after graduating high school, she moved to LA. and became a famous model for Playboy and a Bunny for a fleeting bit of time. Later my Julie hit the big time with a recurring part in the TV show **Growing Pains** as Julie Costello during the 89-90 season. I guess I could say my first girlfriend was Julie McCullough, a really beautiful lady inside and outside luckily for me, we still keep in touch.

I worked at the airline's VIP lounges and often would meet celebrities. Then occasionally I might meet them later at some other event. Arnold Schwarzenegger being one. I had met him while I was competing in bodybuilding, he was always giving positive reinforcement to us competitors. Later I would meet him in the VIP lounge while working. He has always been cordial and greets me in German.

Other people I served were the likes of Howard Cosell, Muhammad Ali, Foster Brooks, Huey Lewis and The News. Billy Joel and David Bowie, Mike Wallace Morley Safer, tennis stars the William sisters even Donald Trump.

I had known Andre the Giant through my friend Kerry. I would always have to get him two belt extenders when he was flying. He was a very large man and always in pain. It always hurt me just to watch him get around knowing he had to live with it too. Way too many years of working the wrestling game left him arthritic, and with bone-on-bone play, because of lost cartilage. Though I must say he actually had a very gentle Soul.

After Dirk Nowitzki's first visit to Dallas, he returned on my flight. He came onboard carrying a huge, framed picture he wanted to take back to Germany with him. I explained to him he could not just hold it.

"Why not?" he asked in very broken English. Then trying to explain who he was.

I answered him in German. "Yes, sir I know who you are, but if the plane hit turbulence and this picture goes flying, it could hurt someone. You do not want that do you?"

He just looked at me surprised I spoke such good German. "I will store this in cargo, and it will be in fine condition when you arrive at your destination."

We spoke for a short while. I asked him how his English lessons were going.

"Not so good" he said, pulling his shoulders up.

"Try watching kid's programs." I suggested," It worked for me."

Lots of Playboy Bunnies rode with us and The Texas Rangers, Cowboys and the Mavericks all chartered with us.

Fate, or Luck: May 25th, 1979, the worst airliner crash in US history happen. An American Airlines DC 10 took off from Chicago heading to Los Angles. Aboard were 273 people. Including 13 crew members. Wheels barely off the ground, the plane's left jet engine dropped off, flipping over on the top of the wing then falling on to the ground. Leaving hydraulics ripped off and a three- foot by three-foot hole in the wing. The whole jumbo jet just flipped over and crashed killing all aboard. One of my closest friends and co-worker, Tony, had been there. Tony had just been bumped off this flight to make room for a group of Playboy Bunnies and some of their corporate executives heading back to LA.

He was sitting in the bar and watching the whole thing, happening just outside the huge glass windows. All he could do is shiver from the knowledge how close he was to having died just a few moments before. **Fate, Luck?**

Chapter 19

The Downside

In 1989 my friend Kerry Von Erich of the famous wrestling family and I began working out at Power House gym when after a few weeks a friend of Kerry's began joining us in our work outs. A really interesting guy by the name James," Jimmy" Bryan Hellwig AKA Ultimate Warrior. We would work out on Mondays, Wednesdays, and Fridays from 6:00 – 8:30 pm. Wednesday though after a heavy work out we would clean up, eat dinner at Furr's cafeteria then go to a club in North Fort Worth called Filthy McNasty. This is where we had the job judging the weekly Wet Tee Shirt contest. An extremely tough job, but then someone had to do it, why not a professional power lifter, and a couple of world-famous wrestlers?

One night after our judging job was completed, we headed down the street to the Cadillac Bar. No sooner had we walk in, then a half-drunk redneck cowboy walks over to me and gets in my face. "I bet I could get big like you if I took a bunch of steroids." I just chuckled and turned away, and he sucker punched me, hitting me, from behind, landing his fist to the side of my face. My eye hurt like hell, but this dumb MF let my DEVIL loose. I hit him so hard his nose exploded under my fist. The police arrived just as I was done. They recognized my companions and guided us out the back door and sent us home. I still had a swollen blacken eye when I went to work and had a lot of explaining to do. Management checked with the police to make sure I had not been arrested or involved in any legal issues. I had to endure a few weeks of embarrassment and much ribbing, for having been sucker punch. Of course, my stock answer was. "This is nothing you should see the other guy." Helped my ego but did nothing for the pain I felt every time I smiled, or frowned, or just about everything I did.

I have been arrested three times each for fighting. Being a man with 23" arms and 36" legs got me in lots of trouble, so sometimes my size could be a curse. A drunken idiot would want to arm wrestle, or just have a fist fight to prove to themselves or their group how tough they were. Or at least how tough they thought they were. If we were arm wrestling, my grip usually was enough to shut some of these yahoo's down, other times I just lock my elbows then just let the other guy waste himself on his initial effort, when he was done, I would just slam their arm down, the look of on their faces of defeat was always sweet to me.

My friend Kerry advised me, "If you got to fight someone, try to throw the first punch, make it count and if you're lucky it may be all you need to throw." Unfortunately, or fortunately, it was true, but throwing the first punch can also land you in jail for the night. I rarely lost, but fighting is not in my nature.

Being a celebrity had other advantages too. We always got backstage passes for musical events like The Texas Jam held in the Cotton Bowl every Fourth of July. At the 1989's event, ESPN was there, and we were all interviewed. The tapes were aired on the following weekend's national sports show. We were strutting around like a bunch of Peacocks and were being offered anything we wanted for free. Food, drinks, drugs. The wrestlers took everything offered, me just some weed and a hit of acid. From Fair Park we all climbed in my truck and headed to Furr's for something to eat. Our group had no sooner sat down to eat, and fellow dinners began coming over. Wanting auto graphs, and to have discussions about this and that. Before we got halfway through our food a growing crowd began filling every available space. We could not even leave it was so packed. The manager called the police, and they helped by escorting us out the back door and to my truck. From there we headed toward Ft. Worth so Kerry and the Ultimate Warrior could score more coke. I was speeding down the highway and nodded off. I just blacked out. The Warrior slapped my shoulder. "Dude, are you there?" I awoke just in time to avoid running into the back of an 18-wheeler while going 70 mph. My **Lady Luck** was still over seeing me.

I pulled off the highway and headed to a friend from work home. I knew he was having a big party and all the drugs these guys would need. We were greeted with open arms. I sat down on a couch and quickly fell asleep. When I woke up the next morning, I was totally nude. I asked my host. "Heah, what the hell happened?"

He just laughed. "Russ, you fell asleep, then got up a few hours later, then took all your clothes off and went back to sleep. You were the hit of the party, along with your giant of friends. Bring them back anytime you want. Those guys really know how party and get crazy."

I passed on several opportunities to go into professional wrestling, a lot of ex-football players do, but that drama was not what I wanted in my life.

Kerry and The Ultimate Warrior started their work out first, with a big fat joint while in the gym's parking lot. After words they would hit a Eightball of Cocaine which is 3- to 3.5 grams of Cocaine, that is lot of cocaine which is also highly addictive. Then they did their two-and-a-half-hour gym work outs. Pressing themselves to the max. Often over doing it and hurting themselves, to the point they then would have to take pain pills for the side effects of the heavy work outs. I may have taken growth hormones and smoked a lot of weed but Thank G-d I never went down that road. In the end those drugs would be used by my friend Kerry just to kill his pain.

One night the two of them came into the Powerhouse Gym in North Richland Hill. As usual they put in their normal heavy work out, but this time, they really were coked up and quite wired. For some reason instead of being exhausted from the work they did it made them get angry. Coke and steroids are not a good combination. They had worked themselves up to create rage, Roid-Rage it is called. They began throwing weights at the glass mirrors along the walls. The more glass they broke the madder they got. When they left, the whole gym was covered with broken glass.

Kerry hired a guy I knew from work, Tommy Gibson to fly every Tuesday from Dallas DFW airport to El- Paso, where Tommy would cross over the border to Ciudad Juarez Mexico. In Mexico, any drug you wanted can be bought in any pharmacy, without a written prescription or anything else, except the cash. Eric would buy the supply of Kerry's drugs, put them in his boots. Walk back across the border. Wearing his airline uniform, he never got stopped. The custom agents would just wave him through. He would come back on a return flight to DFW airport. Deliver his payload to Kerry and walk away with a pocket full of cash.

In 1985 Kerry had his famous motorcycle accident. Where he crashed his bike while being very wired up. Kerry was lucky to have survived, but he did lose a foot. That in its self-did not help his battle with pain relievers, needing them more than ever before.

I must give him credit; despite the physical loss of his foot, he never gave up and kept working out both in the gym and in the ring. He went back to his sport with renewed vigor.

I watched Kerry work hard and with all the different drugs he was able to come back and compete.

He went to work for Vince Mc Mahon, the promoter who had Dwayne, "The Rock" Johnson, Jon Cena, and even Hulk Hogan, now The Texas Tornado, Kerry Von Eric on his venues.

In the end his drug use and his erratic behavior got hm fired. He also had been arrested for spousal abuse of his wife, Kathern Murry, and had been busted and convicted for drug possession, and sales of controlled substance. His next stop was to be Texas State Prison.

Instead of facing his problems head on, Kerry at only 33 years old, choice to kill himself. He took a revolver and shot himself in the heart. He chooses the heart, not the face. Because even in death he had a large ego. He wanted his family to have an open casket, so he did not want his face messed up by a gunshot wound.

The Ultimate Warriors long term drug use, especially cocaine, ended his life at only 55 years old when he suffered a massive heart attack and died.

Fate has always guided me, thank-God. I made the choice to do less pharmaceuticals rather than more.

This was also about the same time American Airlines brought in DEA agents to work as employees and work under cover, to clean up the company's underground drug shipping problems. Tommy was one of the first to be arrested.

I had been working side by side with a guy named David Sampson for over six months. He was a great worker, and I really thought he was going to be my next big success story. It turned out David was a plant and a senior officer in the DEA. Several people I knew were arrested, I thought, had not been involved in any of that kind of activity. I just kept my head down and continued doing my job as usual.

Chapter 20

My Reality

If I had the choice to do things differently, would I have?

If I knew what I know now would I have chosen different paths?

What I do know is, I sincerely regret the pain I have caused others.

I am most thankful for my family who were there for me during my worst of times.

I am ecstatic for every day that I do have.

Today I know who I am, my weaknesses and my strengths.

I wish to share my journey with others who may find hope and encouragement from my life's story.

It all began with her.

Chapter 21

My New Life's Purpose

Cannabises has been part of my life since I was a kid. But now my investigation brought me to a deep look into this miracle plant, which led me to FECO or Full Extract Canna Oil = whole plant extract. From root to flower and everything between. The process combines molecules and terpenes from various parts of the plant, to create the most versatile healing, thick oil. When processed you had A Whole Plant Extract. By using different plants with different terps or not from a Cannabis plant but also the sister plant, Hemp. Which is a plant with more CBD molecules for a different end product with more CBD now being the base ingredient. Both forms of FECO are a significant help to their educated consumers.

After only four months of my new regiment, less than six months after I was sent home to die, I was boarding a plane with my wife, heading to Germany to visit family, then on to Budapest, last stop Austria. Before heading back home. Spreading the word of my incredible life's journey, my story. To hungry for information audiences.

PAIN IS MY COMPANION

 **Russell Langhammer**
Patient Advocate at State of Texas
now · 🌐

Doctors gave me only months to live in 2019... I had 5 way open heart ❤️ bypass surgery and received my 4th pacemaker... then, I started using RSO FECO and Psylocybin mushrooms 🍄 and I am back Ya'll ! My wife and I travel around the world 🌍 now telling people how I came back from the dying and got back up and started living again thanks to Cannabis concentrates and Fungus ! 😏... we just got back from Cabo San Lucas and I actually got to fish 🐟 again like I did before disability...
LIFE IS AWESOME AGAIN 👌
#FREETHEWEEDTEXAS
#cannabis #people #travel # #doctors #surgery #CABOCANNABISCOMPANY #NEVERGIVEUP #IMBACK

Endocannabinoid system

The endocannabinoid system is a biological system composed of endocannabinoids, which are endogenous lipid-based retrograde neurotransmitters that bind to cannabinoid receptors, and cannabinoid receptor proteins that are expressed throughout the vertebrate central nervous system and peripheral nervous system. Wikipedia

Feeding the body's endocannabinoid system is as important as feeding a person's stomach. In days of olds, pre- WR Hurst. Hemp and cannabises were grown for cheap feed for cows, chickens, horses. We would eat the meat, eggs, milk and in doing so get our bodies needed cannonades to feed our bodies endocannabinoid system.

When our bodies are not fed these cannonades our body suffers in many ways, we are only just now beginning to discover.

A few things have been found out. Low or no feeding of this system will lower a body's pain thresh hold. That was all I needed to know, I was going to feed mine, more than just one way. I added Pasteurized fresh eggs, flax seeds and its oil, chia seeds, [without the pet] walnuts and sardines and anchovies, which I kind of grown to like. Plus, FECO every day.

My story and telling it has become my new life's goal, to spread the word of mother nature's pain relievers and her many wonderful healing properties, which are available to us all.

Texas Marijuana Policy Lobby Day
February 7th, 2019

Cannabis had been an important part of my pain management regiment, and it also opens my mind to view life differently. I began to meet different people who like me were proponents of freeing the Weed in Texas as it was being legalized in more and more states. I began telling my own story to people, realizing my story was an important one to share. I began to get requests to spread the truth and tell my tale at venues in Texas and beyond in years to come.

Fellow cancer survivor because of FECO.

The Best Man I have ever known.

Coach Gayle Kingery

Coach Kingery's/ My Work Out Routine:

Always start with a walk to warm up and stretch muscles on a treadmill, or outside weather permitting.
Then lungers with weights, Extensions, and Presses.
Work Legs, Back, and Triceps. On Mondays and Fridays.
Biceps, Chest, and the rest of my body Wednesdays.

The routine I used during Power Lifting/Body Building while competing.

Every day: Warm up first.
Mondays: Chest and Shoulders.
Tuesdays: Back and Biceps.
Wednesday: Legs and Abs. @ least 3 hours or preferably until you can't push yourself anymore.
Thursday: Repeat Mondays work out.
Every day: Stomach and Caves.
Weekends. "As much cardio as possible as hard as possible, one can never get too much of this.

Accomplishments:

My wining Squat Weight= 802 pounds
My wining Bench Weight= 560 pounds
My wining Dead Weight= 725 pounds
1993 I won first place in the 242 # class.
1994 I won first place in the 220# class.

RETIRED from Competition end of 1994.

The Final Chapter

I have learned a few things on my life's journey.

First it is never over until you say it is over or until the good lord says so.

Each of us must find our true self and put effort into being the person you want to be through actual action. What those actions are define who you really will be.

I deeply believe when you are ready, the right people will come into your life.

Which comes with my last observation.

Marriage is tough, work is tough, life is tough. Everything we do in one way, or another is a choice, of which tough choice/road we will choose. Always pick the one with the best outcome, not the easiest.

My advice to you all is free.

My story now told I end by thanking you for having taken the time to read this book of my life's journey.

Russell, Rusty, Langhammer

Other books by Steve Kravetz

Fictions:

A Marijuana Man: A coming of age story of the 1960's.

The Bastardo: Mid 1800's Sicily. The beginning of the Mafia.

The Bastardos: Part two: The saga of the Alliance.

Non-Fiction Book:

The Tales of The Tails Every Rescue Dog Has a Story.

Ghost Written Book:

Pain Is My Companion

authorstevekravetz.com

Award winning storyteller.

Steve Kravetz

www.ingramcontent.com/pod-product-compliance
Lightning Source LLC
Chambersburg PA
CBHW070737020526
44118CB00035B/1427